THE
SEVENTH
MILLENNIUM

A Look at
Life's Possibilities in the New Age
Before Us

LUKE LEA

In Jewish lore there is an old and decidedly secular version of the millennial idea according to which the human race, after laboring six thousand years in servitude, will achieve a thousand years of political and economic freedom. The Great Sabbath, as the rabbis called it, would be an age of leisure and equality shared by all the peoples of the world.[*]

"If you will it, it is no dream."

—Theodor Herzl

---

[*] See Louis Ginsberg, The Legends of the Jews, Jewish Publication Society, volume 5, p. 128.

Contents

Preface

The ideal of a simple life on the land, the vision of a new day *'when every man will sit under his own vine, and nation shall not vex nation anymore'*—these are, perhaps, as old as history, and as broad as humankind. Yet seldom if ever I suspect has the ideal been so apt, or the vision more compelling, than they are today, when thanks to the great Tree of Capital we have for the first time not only the means to realize the dream in substance if we choose, but also the means to destroy ourselves in the event we should fail. In a sense, then, we may already be living in the judgment day. The only question is, Shall we try to go on living the way we do now in a world divided between the strong and the weak, the rich and the poor, the educated and the ignorant: a foolish, dangerously imbalanced world whose symptoms include the mass migrations of peoples across international boundaries, social and cultural disintegration throughout the former lands of Christendom, and un-supportable levels of debt almost everywhere we look, the sum of which can only end in violence and decay? Or shall we strive to seek a fairer and more permanent form of civilization based on a just division of the world's desserts, with equitable portions of liberty, leisure, and the good things of this earth for all people everywhere?

It is against the background of this question that I originally wrote and now have gathered together these notes towards a new way of life in America, not so much hoping as actually believing that the best of them at least, despite their many shortcomings and the unresolved issues they raise, were going to prove useful in the period ahead. But of course only time will tell whether this faith that I placed in the seemingly simple idea I was writing about—an idea so beautiful, I felt, that it had to be true—was justified or not.

Hunt Park
August 7, 2020

Chapter One
A Good Place to Live

Then I saw "a new heaven and a new earth," for the first heaven and the first earth had passed away [1]

In July of 1976, in the midst of America's Bicentennial celebrations, the Gallup organization sent its team of pollsters into the field to conduct face-to-face interviews with a cross section of the American public. One of the questions asked was the following:

> *As a new way to live in America, the idea has been suggested of building factories in rural areas—away from cities—and running them on part-time jobs. Under this arrangement the man and the woman would each work 3 days a week 6 hours a day. People would have enough spare time to build their own houses, to cultivate a garden and for hobbies and other outside interests.*

> *How interested would you be in this way of life?*

Forty percent of those interviewed answered either "definitely" or "probably" with another twenty-five percent indicating that they might possibly be interested.

THE SEVENTH MILLENNIUM

Those were remarkably high numbers. Even more remarkable, they turned out to be broadly representative of the country as a whole when broken down by race, gender, age group, family income, and years of education. (See Appendix I for a complete copy of the Gallup report, *The Public's Attitudes Towards a New Way to Live in America.*)

But what I find most remarkable about those results is that they came at the very height of America's middle-class prosperity, during a time when the American dream of a house in the suburbs and a full-time mom who stayed at home with the kids was still within reach of the average working-class family, which of course is no longer the case. One can only wonder what the numbers might be if that same question were repeated today.

In any case, those old poll results have been largely forgotten. The only reason I remember them is that I happen to have been the young man at the time who commissioned the question on which they were based, having promised my family that I would give up on the idea if no one were interested in living this way. I did not give up needless to say, which may help to explain how the following collection of notes can fairly be described as the fruit of a lifetime of research and reflection all revolving around one central idea: the idea of factories in the countryside run on part-time jobs and what they might mean for the world that we live in.

A GOOD PLACE TO LIVE

ii

Now just to be clear, by *in the countryside* I mean in places that are well out beyond the exurban fringe of the nearest metropolitan area.[2] And by *run on part-time jobs* I mean that most of the people employed in these factories—all those doing routine wage work—will be on the job four to six hours a day, three or four days a week.[3] As we shall see in the next chapter, there is every reason to believe that there are many kinds of factories in the United States today (I say many kinds, not all) that can be made to run considerably faster and more efficiently this way than when they are manned by a full-time workforce, thereby generating a higher rate of return on investment. This point is crucial, as I hardly need emphasize.

But in this introduction I want to focus not so much on the factories themselves—which are, after all, but the means to an end—as on the new kinds of small country towns that might develop around them and on the new lifestyle that would become possible for the working men and women who live in these towns.

The new lifestyle itself is easy enough to imagine. Being employed away from home so few hours in the week, working people will have a great deal more free time at their disposal than they do today: time that they can use to do things directly for themselves and each other which now they pay others to do in their stead. You could call it a compromise—or, better yet, a trade-off—

between the age-old longing for the simple life and the technological imperatives of a modern industrial society.

But whichever you choose to call it, I would like to spend the remainder of this chapter sketching a few of what I believe to be its most important natural advantages, giving special attention to the ways that it would enable ordinary working people to make a much more efficient use of their limited time and resources to satisfy their human needs.

iii

Let me start with the human individual, that central figure in Western civilization, whose present and future happiness are the true measures of its worth. She (or he, as the case may be) will begin to enjoy a great deal more personal freedom than the common man or woman has ever enjoyed since history and civilization began; and along with her newfound freedom she will experience a corresponding enlargement in the scope and variety of activities that compose her working day. Instead of being confined to the narrow routines of a nine-to-five job, she will find herself spending fully half her working life as her own person, leading a far more varied and independent existence than is possible today—an existence, let me note, that is much closer in spirit to the one in which we evolved as a species and to which, presumably, we are adapted by nature.[4] I sometimes wonder if this is the life to which scripture refers, where it is written:

Thou hast left thy first love; remember, therefore, from whence thou art fallen.[5]

I also wonder if it is merely a coincidence that the three main areas of human activity that have most stubbornly resisted the techniques of modern mass production, yielding to them only grudgingly and with generally inferior results—I refer to the building of our houses, to the preparation and serving of the food that we eat, and to the daily care of the young and the old—are also the areas that are, or can be, most intrinsically rewarding: that afford us with opportunities to satisfy our basic human instinct for workmanship, to express ourselves with the work of our hands, and to exercise our manifold human capacity for love and affection.

I do not know the answer to these questions. But I do know that compared to the way we live now, the new way of life I am proposing in these pages will make the pursuit of happiness in America a far more agreeable enterprise for those of our citizens who might choose it, and one with far better prospects of success.

THE SEVENTH MILLENNIUM

iv

So much then for the happiness of the individual. Let us turn next to the family to which he belongs, a family being not only the oldest and most universal of all human institutions but also the one that is primarily responsible for the acculturation of our children—and hence for the transmission of those sentiments and ideals that lie at the heart of our democratic society and its liberal institutions, whose preservation for the enjoyment of this and future generations we hold to be a sacred trust. How might the American family fare under this new dispensation?

Let me start with the obvious. Parents will be spending a lot more time in the company of their children and each other than is possible today, and they will be doing things together besides watching television or playing computer games while plunked on the couch. As a simple matter of necessity home and hearth will become once more what traditionally they always were: a scene of useful domestic activity and a setting in which every family member has a role to play and real responsibilities to meet.

There will certainly be no shortage of quality time between parents and children the way there is now, whether it take place in the course of preparing meals together on a more regular basis, while sitting around the family dinner table, or as they go about the many other commonplace chores of everyday life. Opportunities are sure to abound not only for parents to joke and play around with their kids but to engage them in more serious conversations about the important things in life whenever the situation warrants or the occasion seems appropriate. In such simple ways as these we can confidently predict that the American family will be restored, not only as a functioning economic unit, but in its age-old role of nurture and support.

Something similar can be predicted for the institution of marriage upon which the social stability of the biological family depends. The bonds of matrimony are certain to grow stronger once the combined earnings of two part-time working adults are required to maintain an independent household. Contrast that to the situation so common today in which both parents are employed full-time outside the home and can therefore afford to live on their own if and when they so choose. Small wonder so many marriages now end in divorce! But under the terms of the new arrangement I am describing here the decision to walk out on a marriage becomes a far less convenient option, which means that fewer married couples are likely to go through the trauma of a divorce with all that this implies for the emotional security, material well-being, and future happiness of their children, to say nothing of their own.

THE SEVENTH MILLENNIUM

V

As long as we are on the subject of domestic institutions, let me to suggest the possibility of reverting to a more traditional, three-generation form of the family—not under one roof however (let us be clear about that), but rather under two, at opposite ends of the garden. The advantages of this arrangement would arise as a simple function of proximity. Grandparents, once they live close by, will be in a position to help look after their grandchildren—while they are still infants and toddlers especially—on those occasions that invariably arise when both parents have to be away from home at the same time. Then, later on in life, when the grandparents themselves have grown old and feeble and are no longer be able to live on their own, their children and grandchildren will be near enough to help look after them.

As a possible alternative to day care and nursing homes such a new three-generation form of the family deserves serious attention. For not only would it offer a far more natural and humane way to solve these two age-old problems of care, but it promises a solution that from a purely financial point of view would be infinitely more affordable for the average working-class family.

Which brings us to the whole issue of retirement. As most Americans know by now, our Social Security system is on a financially unsustainable path. The aging of the baby-boom generation combined with the fact that people today are both living longer and having fewer children than they did in the past, has resulted in a situation in which the number of new retirees who are drawing money out of the Social Security trust fund is growing considerably faster than the number of new workers who are paying money in. What this portends, all experts agree, is one or more of the following three possibilities: either the Social Security payroll tax, which is already consuming more than twelve percent of workers' wages, must go up another five or six points; or the age at which workers become eligible for full Social Security benefits, which has already risen from sixty-five to sixty-seven, must continue to rise to well beyond seventy; or monthly cash benefits must be substantially reduced. None of these alternatives is politically palatable to say the very least.

But under the terms of the new way of life that I am here proposing this dilemma will largely disappear. That is to say, once work and leisure are thoroughly integrated into the fabric of everyday life people will no longer feel the same *need* to retire that they do today. Instead of exiting the workforce completely once they reach a certain predetermined age, older workers will be able to

9

gravitate to easier kinds of employment for even shorter periods of time: twelve hours a week behind a checkout counter, for instance, instead of eighteen to twenty-four hours on an assembly line. And when eventually they do reach that stage in life when they are no longer physically or mentally capable of holding down a real paying job, then, as we just saw, they need no longer depend upon their Social Security checks alone to meet all of their material needs. Which means that their benefits can be lower without compromising the quality of their lives.

There is one last advantage to this three-generation form of the family that I would like to touch upon briefly, one that would arise only at the very end of life when one's bodily organs begin to fail and death makes its final approach. When that day inevitably rolls round, instead of being carted off to a nursing home or hospital at enormous public expense, the dying person could remain at home with the help of professionally trained hospice workers, which the public could provide at a small fraction of the cost. How much better to die that way, at home in one's bed, surrounded by the voices of loved ones, than alone in an institution somewhere at the mercy of strangers!

vii

Having considered both the happiness of the individual and the welfare of his or her family, let us turn

10

next to the neighborhoods in which these families will dwell, a neighborhood being (after the family itself) the second oldest and most universal of all human institutions, corresponding as it does to the primitive band and to the ancient and medieval village. What new kinds of neighborhoods might we expect to see under this new dispensation, and how might they differ from the ones most of us grew up in?

Here again I will begin with the obvious. We are going to be seeing many more adults out and about during the regular course of the week. With so much of their lives now centered round their homes and their gardens this is a forgone conclusion. Grown-ups will be visible on a daily basis engaged in a variety of useful activities, whether it be something as simple as tending a garden or mending a broken home appliance, or something as complex as a major home addition. The neighborhood, in other words, will no longer be the deserted village most of us grew up in, which is what you get when most of the grown-ups climb into their automobiles five days a week and drive away to a full-time job.

For the children in the neighborhood this will be a decided advantage. For it means that henceforth they will be exposed to the adult world of work at an earlier age and to a far greater extent than is possible in a society in which most real work is done away from home and out of the sight of children. And being the curious creatures they are, these neighborhood children are bound to pick up useful skills and gain some practical knowledge in the

11

natural course of growing up—at first by looking, later on by asking, and finally by lending a helping hand—thereby acquiring a fund of valuable experience that will stand them in good stead in their lives ahead.

What is more, those very same adults we just saw out in their yards on a daily basis will be well positioned to keep a collective eye on all the children in the neighborhood as they run and play among the houses, warning them away from danger, keeping them out of mischief, and thereby providing a useful extension to the family itself.

Familiar faces in familiar places, in short, are going to make these neighborhoods of the future into far safer as well as far more congenial environments for children and grown-ups alike.

viii

Nor should we overlook the many other opportunities for sharing that will naturally present themselves. With so many adults now at home so much of the time it becomes a simple matter of convenience to go next door or down the street to borrow a cup of sugar or seek a helping hand. Visiting and casual hospitality are sure to become more common once friends and neighbors begin to avail themselves of some of their newfound leisure. Or consider such a simple possibility as a neighborhood post office: a covered pavilion instead of

12

individual mailboxes in front of each house. Not only would this save considerable time and expense for the postal delivery services, but it would provide a convenient spot where neighbors would be likely to run into one another on a daily basis, exchange local gossip, and pass along any news that might be of interest.

Taking these possibilities a step further, the families in a neighborhood might elect to go in together to purchase a small garden tractor with which they could till up their gardens in the spring and fall, thereby saving them all a good deal of time and effort. Or they might choose—or, rather, as we shall soon see, they may virtually be forced—to organize neighborhood house-building parties in the old Midwestern barn-raising tradition, which turns out to be an effective as well as a highly enjoyable way to navigate some of the earliest and most difficult stages of construction. And of course they could institute annual neighborhood picnics on Labor Day and the Fourth of July, which is a time-tested way to foster good neighborly feelings and a sense of local solidarity.

ix

Let us turn next to the subject of neighborhood planning. What would be the best way to arrange the houses in a neighborhood if our goal is to maximize the opportunities for sharing such as the ones I have just been describing? Here I think there are some lessons to be learned from the New Urbanism movement that is already underway in certain parts of the United States.[6]

For one thing, we could break the habit of building our houses along both sides of the street like so many beads on a string. The alternative is to arrange them around a central open area—a village green or neighborhood commons, if you will—which would serve both as a pocket park for the grown-ups and a playground for the kids. (see figure 1).

Another custom we might get away from is that of locating our houses far back from the street in order to make room for expansive front lawns. The alternative here is to place them close to the street, facing the park, and to give them wide front porches as was the custom in many working- and middle-class neighborhoods before the advent of the high-speed automobile. The advantage of this arrangement lies in the fact that it makes for easy line-of-sight communication between the adults in the house and the children who are playing across the street, as well as between people sitting on their porches and anyone who happens to be walking or bicycling by.

I might mention that this is roughly the way the houses were arranged in Ferger Place, which is the name of the neighborhood where I grew up in Chattanooga, Tennessee. Among the families who lived in Ferger Place it was reputed to be (though I doubt this is true) the oldest planned neighborhood community south of the Mason–Dixon line.

A GOOD PLACE TO LIVE

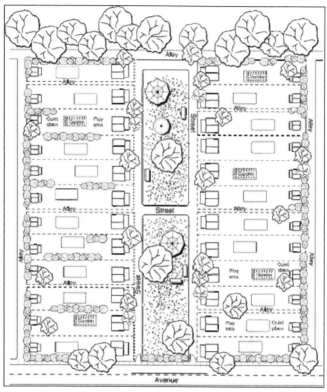

Figure 1

x

Now, to be sure, if the houses are to be set forward on their lots instead of back from the street, and assuming they are not far apart, this means that the gardens will have to be located behind, in long back yards that would stretch from the rear of each main house, in which the parents and their children will live, to the more modest quarters at the far end of the garden where the grandparents will be, those quarters themselves being accessible by an alleyway that runs across the backs of the lots (see figure 2). The advantage of this arrangement is that it would define a space—bounded by the larger house in front and the smaller one at the rear of the garden—of relative peace and quiet, a place not open to the street, where a person could sit and read, or meditate, or sing the baby to sleep, and not be bothered. As for the size of each family's homestead, I would imagine no more than an acre (or roughly the size of a football field) but not less than half an acre.

A GOOD PLACE TO LIVE

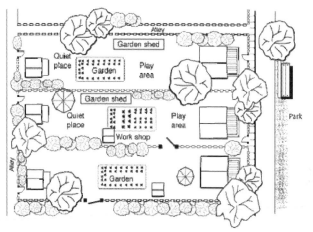

Figure 2

Beyond the bounds of the local neighborhood community and completely surrounding it is where the rest of the new town would lie, a town being the smallest independent political unit under our system of government and the third circle of development without which no rural society is truly complete.

Ideally what would one of these new towns look like? How big should it be in terms of population and geographical extent? How should the neighborhoods be arranged in relation to each other and to the other parts of town where people will work and do most of their shopping? Where will the schools and churches be located? Will there be easy access to the open countryside? How about to the nearest big city? All these and many other questions besides will have to be answered one way or another.

Like most of the ideas in this book, the ideal solution I am about to describe is not original with me. In fact, it is little more than an updated and slightly modified version of the garden city concept as it was first formulated in England over a century ago, where it inspired an English town-planning movement. [7] The Victorian gentleman who originated the concept was Ebenezer Howard, an amateur town planner (there were no professionals back then) whose declared intention and clearly stated goal was simplicity itself: to combine the best features of city and country living while taking steps to avoid their worst disadvantages.

Thus Howard noted that real estate is extraordinarily expensive in a big city but almost ridiculously cheap by comparison in rural areas that are far from the nearest big city. Big cities are filled with anonymous strangers whom one has no way of knowing, let alone trusting, whereas in small country towns the inhabitants generally recognize one another on sight and wear their reputations on their sleeves. Big cities provide more opportunities for employment and a much wider variety of places to shop, but in a blighted landscape largely devoid of the beauties of nature. The downtown of a big city in particular is almost invariably a noisy, polluted, and highly congested space where just getting around can be a frustrating experience. The distances between work and home are several times longer in big cities than in small country towns, and the costs of personal transportation (in time as well as in money) are correspondingly higher. Compared to a small town, big-city politics are highly opaque; the stakes are much higher and the opportunities for graft and corruption are far more abundant. In fact, the average citizen in a big city stands little chance of exercising his vote in any meaningful way.

Yet for all these disadvantages, Howard acknowledged that big cities also enjoyed certain crucial advantages when it came to the number and quality of their educational institutions, the variety of their theaters and places of entertainment, the size of their libraries, the quality of their museums, and the general range of social and cultural opportunities that they were able to provide. The highly educated or otherwise exceptional individual stands a far better chance of meeting his counterpart in a big city than in a small country town.

Given this list of advantages and disadvantages, just how did Howard propose to combine the best of both worlds? The answer, he declared, was to design and build a new kind of town that would occupy the middle ground or "sweet spot" between these extremes: a moderately sized municipality of some twenty-five thousand inhabitants that would be set down in the middle of the open countryside. And to make sure that these new "garden cities," as he called them, would forever remain in that sweet spot, he stipulated that certain definite measures be taken to prevent their ever growing beyond it.

xii

I shall return in a moment to just what those measures were, but first I want to describe the initial sequence of steps as Howard laid them out, by which an organized group might go about creating one of these garden cities from scratch.

The first step, naturally enough, would be to identify and acquire a suitable town site: a contiguous tract of land in the rural countryside of some twenty-five thousand acres in total extent (or approximately one acre for each future inhabitant). It would be absolutely essential, Howard never ceased to emphasize, that this site be located far enough away from the nearest big city to place it completely outside the orbit of urban real estate speculation. Then, and only then, would it be possible to purchase the property at its true agricultural value, which is to say at a price low enough that its agricultural productivity alone—whether employed as farmland, woodland, or pasture—would generate enough income to cover the mortgage for an indefinite period of time.

Once a suitable site had been identified and purchased (I shall return to how the purchase might be financed in chapter four), Howard stipulated that fully half the site be set aside as a permanent "greenbelt" (he invented the term) that would completely envelop the future municipality and be held in its trust. This surrounding greenbelt would serve two essential purposes. First, it would establish the community's identity as a distinct town in the countryside. And second, it would constitute an insuperable physical barrier that would shield the town from the encroachment of all forms of future urban overdevelopment, whether arising from forces within the community or outside its borders. Boulder, Colorado, furnishes an excellent example of such a greenbelt today.

Meanwhile, the other half of the land, the half completely surrounded by the greenbelt, is where the town proper would be constructed. Only within this central core area would the town's future inhabitants actually reside, work, and go about their daily lives. Figure 3 is a rough diagram of what the whole thing would look like:

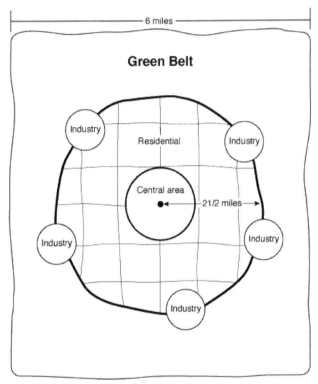

Figure 3

There are a couple of things to notice about this arrangement. One is the placement of the industrial parks in which the factories will be located. They form a discontinuous set of islands on the outer fringes of the residential zone. I emphasize the word *discontinuous* here because the aim is to avoid a continuous wall of industrial development that would cut the town off, both visually and physically, from the surrounding greenbelt and the open countryside beyond. The aim, in other words, is to preserve the rural feel of the place to the maximum possible degree.

The second thing to notice is the central location of the downtown commercial area. The goal here is to minimize the distances between work and home and the place where families will do most of their shopping. Together with the small radius of the town itself, this highlights one of the motivating features shaping this updated version of Howard's original garden city concept, namely, to design a community in which high-speed automobiles are no longer an everyday necessity. In their place lightweight, low-speed electric cars and trucks or their motorized equivalents would become the town's primary mode of personal transportation.

Had I drawn this diagram in greater detail, one would be able to discern a number of small grammar schools and convenience stores embedded in the residential matrix. Here the aim is to eliminate the need for motorized transport in any form, in this case by making it easy for young children to either walk or bike to the nearest neighborhood school, as could their parents and grandparents whenever they need to go on minor shopping expeditions.

Even if we assume that people in the towns will occasionally need to rent high-speed automobiles in order to get into the nearest big city, it should be obvious that the average family's spending on personal transportation will be a small fraction of what it is today. For two reasons: *First*, because the total number of miles driven in a year will be several times lower. And *second*, because on a per-mile basis, lightweight, low-speed vehicles are much cheaper to purchase, insure, fuel, and maintain than today's high-speed automobiles. We need to keep these two facts in mind when it comes time to estimate what a future family's real standard of living will be. Transportation, after all, is the means to an end; it is a cost, in other words, not an end in itself, a point that is too often overlooked.

xiv

Let us now turn our attention to the central downtown area, which is where the town's residents will do most of their shopping. Howard proposed that the municipality retain title to all of the commercial real estate within its boundaries, using the revenues generated by rents and leases on that real estate (which would be equivalent to a tax on what Henry George famously called "the unearned increment"[8]) to finance local government. Whether this is a necessary or wholly practicable idea I am not prepared to say. In any case, it is with issues of

24

form and function, not public finance, that I am here most concerned. How big should the downtown be? How should it be laid out? And, above all, what purposes should it serve?

The principal point I wish to make is that the new downtown should be more than just a place where people can shop. Like the agora in ancient Greek city-states, it should also serve as the center of the town's social and political life. Or to choose an example much closer to home, it should be laid out in such a fashion as to foster that spirit of local self-government which Alexis de Tocqueville descried in the townships of early nineteenth-century New England, and which he rightly identified as one of the cornerstones of American democracy:

> *The native of New England is attached to his township because it is independent and free: his cooperation in its affairs insures his attachment to its interest; the well being it affords him secures his affection; and its welfare is the aim of his ambition and of his future exertions . . . . [T]he township serves as a center for the desire of public esteem, the want of exciting interests, and the taste for popularity and authority in the midst of the ordinary relations of life; and the passions which commonly embroil society, change their character when they find a vent so near the domestic hearth and the family circle.*[9]

THE SEVENTH MILLENNIUM

How might we envision such civic space today? A traditional town square is certainly one possibility, and there is no question that town squares have a number of points in their favor, not the least being the way they bring a town's public affairs into close proximity with its private commercial activities. But for sheer convenience in all kinds of weather nothing can beat James Rouse's original concept of an indoor shopping mall.[10] Let us therefore contemplate something in between: a new hybrid architectural form combining the best features of a traditional town square with the advantages of an enclosed or semi-enclosed shopping galleria.

This new hybrid architectural form, at least as I envision it, would have at its center an open town square not unlike an Italian piazza: an area just big enough to accommodate the town's entire population on those special occasions when the whole community's presence is needed. Around the perimeter of this open space the major public buildings would be arranged: the mayor's office, the local courthouse, a chamber in which the town's council would meet, the local jail, and all the other buildings one normally associates with local self-government. The community's principal place of worship should also be there, it being the one institution that can cement a town's sense of itself as a permanent community. Just behind these public buildings I envision covered porticos shading the entranceways into large enclosed spaces that would house several major discount stores (Home Depot, Lowe's, Target, and the like), two or

26

three grocery chains (enough for price competition), and a variety of smaller retail shops, cafes, private offices, kiosks, and the like.

Parking ideally would be underground or in multi-level parking garages. For that way, instead of being surrounded by acres of asphalt the way modern shopping malls are now, the town's center could be enclosed in a large public park such as Frederick Law Olmsted[11] might have designed: a park complete with greenswards, garden paths, picnic areas, water features, outdoor cafes, a merry-go-round and a Ferris wheel perhaps, even an ice skating rink and a public swimming pool, plus plenty of park benches. The idea would be to create an attractive natural landscape that all the townspeople would necessarily traverse on their way to town: a place where old people can sit and watch the world go by, where teenagers can congregate, young couples court, and whole families relax during their weekly shopping expeditions.

xv

Now our critics will argue that such a hybrid architectural form, no matter how well executed, cannot possibly rival the range of opportunities one finds in a big city. And no doubt our critics will be right to a certain extent.

On the other hand, we can point to a number of offsetting technological developments that have taken

27

place over the course of the last several decades. Thanks to the Internet and United Parcel Service (UPS), it is now possible to obtain on short notice just about any article of merchandise for sale anywhere in the United States or Canada. Services like Netflix, iTunes, and Amazon.com make a virtually unlimited selection of books, movies, and musical offerings available for instant download. Google and Wikipedia put at our fingertips, at absolutely no charge, a range of information, out-of-print books, newspapers, periodicals, images, and video content that until recently only the largest libraries in the world could supply. Our best universities are now posting many of their courses online. And on top of it all, email and the new social media now make it possible to communicate in real time with people all over the world who happen to share our own particular interests, no matter how peculiar or obscure they may be.

Big cities, in short, are rapidly losing many of the advantages that they have traditionally enjoyed. Hick towns across America can now boast better access to a broader range of commercial and cultural resources than even New York City could provide a generation ago. For the first time in history an individual living in the provinces can cultivate his mind just as conveniently as he can cultivate his garden.

Voltaire would be astonished.

Chapter Two
What Profit It?

For unto every one that hath shall be given, but from him that hath not shall be taken away even that which he hath.[12]

Western civilization, of which America is a part, is a civilization based upon capitalism, in which the pursuit of private gain is the motive force that drives the economy and shapes the patterns of its historical development. This is one of the fundamental facts of life, and anyone who proposes to bring about a fundamental reformation in the way we live and work in the West must take it into account. Those who fail to do so either out of ignorance or because they imagine that there must be some way around it are destined to be sadly disappointed, as generations of would-be reformers before us have learned the hard way.

Indeed, it would be hard to list all the projects of reform that have foundered on this bitter truth (I say *bitter* because the history of capitalism has not been a pretty one). Here in America, it would probably begin with our Puritan forefathers who in the first half of the seventeenth century set out to build "a city on a hill" in the wilderness of North America that would be free of all such worldly concerns, not realizing that commerce with the old world they left behind would turn out to be one of the mainstays of their economic existence.[13] It would certainly include a score of utopian socialist experiments, some of them quite famous (Brook Farm in Massachusetts and New Harmony, Indiana are two that come readily to mind) that were organized across the United States in the middle decades of the nineteenth century.[14] And, of course, it would have to include that far more tragic attempt to abolish capitalism altogether in accordance with the dictates of the Marxist–Leninist ideology that was so dogmatically pursued across Europe (and in much of Asia, Africa, and Latin America as well) throughout the greater part of the twentieth century.[15] To this list we can also add a dozen or more doctrinaire left-wing kibbutzim that were established in Palestine in the first half of the last century as part of the Zionist movement to resettle that land, to say nothing of all the sloppy, drug-addled hippie communes of my youth.

Is there nothing good to be gotten from this four-hundred-year-long record of failure? No way to redeem all the pain and frustration felt by so many well-intentioned and for the most part good-hearted souls, including my own dear father, a Norman Thomas–style democratic socialist of considerable intelligence and unusual integrity who suffered the misfortune of having never read Adam Smith in college? As a matter of fact, I think there is a way. We can profit from their experience and at the same time honor their memory by taking a far more realistic approach from the outset, a conclusion that even my father eventually came around to accepting after a quarter century of good-natured debate around the family dinner table.

ii

In other words, if we seriously hope to see factories in the countryside run on part-time jobs here in America anytime soon then we had better be prepared to persuade hardheaded businessmen that it will be in their interests to build them. What case can we make?

Let me begin with a simple thought experiment. Imagine you are the owner of a factory engaged in the manufacture of some product or other. It might be a tangible commodity, something you can touch or hold in your hands, or it might be something intangible such as processing insurance claims. But whatever the product, let us assume the market for it is big enough to justify the techniques of modern mass production: the use of machinery, a high division of labor, standardization of parts, and economies of scale. More specifically, we shall assume that significant quantities of both labor and capital are employed in the manufacturing process and that the pace of production can be adjusted within certain well-defined limits. As long as these last two conditions are met, we shall argue that a factory run on part-time jobs can be made to run significantly faster and more efficiently than an otherwise identical facility manned by a full-time workforce, in which case it will generate a significantly higher rate of return on investment. For two reasons:

First, because workers can work faster and more efficiently for shorter periods of time than for longer, just as in track-and-field the short-distance runners always run faster than the long-distance runners.

And *second*, because these part-time workers will, if anything, be given slightly fewer hours in the week than they might prefer, which means they will be eager to earn every penny they can. Provided their wages are either made proportional to their output or are otherwise tied to their output by some equitable formula to which both sides agree—a crucial proviso to which I shall return at the end of this chapter—it follows that the factory's workforce will be motivated to exert itself both physically and mentally to the maximum possible degree.

For convenience, I shall use the phrase *incentive-based work sprints* to denote this combination of a much shorter workweek and pay tied to output. Our argument then reduces to two closely related propositions: first, that incentive-based work sprints will enable a given manufacturing facility to boost output per man-hour; and second, that such a boost in productivity, even when shared between labor and capital, translates automatically into a higher rate of return on investment. This in a nutshell is the argument we shall make, which I have presented here in a way that I think most businessmen will intuitively understand.

In support of this general conclusion, let me recount a couple of anecdotes. Shortly after I first formulated the argument in this intuitive way—I remember it was right after I got married in February of 1980—I presented it in a letter that I cheekily overnighted to the chief executive officer of the Fantus Company, America's premier management consulting firm in the field of industrial relocation. Two days later, the executive vice president of Fantus flew down to Chattanooga from company headquarters in New Jersey to meet with me, hoping no doubt to have a lead on a possible new source of business. I will never forget the look on his face when he discovered that so far from my being a conventional businessman in coat and tie, I was just an ordinary gardener with mud on my shoes.

The following week, I overnighted the same letter to another leading firm in the field of industrial relocation, this one with offices in midtown Manhattan. Two days later one of the partners in the firm called me on the telephone to discuss what I had written in my letter. I can still remember his exact words when toward the end of a twenty-minute conversation in the course of which I elaborated the argument in much greater detail and answered a number of questions he had, he blurted out in his New York accent, "This is a doable idea, not pie in the sky."

THE SEVENTH MILLENNIUM

It was at that point that I knew I had the formula I was looking for: a succinct, intuitively persuasive argument in favor of factories in the countryside run on part-time jobs that ordinary businessmen could understand.

iii

Even so, it will be useful if I restate the argument in a less intuitive but far more rigorous way, this time using the language of economics and physiology (including neurophysiology). Readers who are not themselves manufacturers or academic economists may find this to be a needlessly abstract way to arrive at the same conclusion. If so, they can safely skip ahead to the next note without missing anything essential. Those who are manufacturers, on the other hand, or who are employed by corporations engaged in manufacturing, will find that a close reading of the following restatement will repay them with some valuable insights into the whole field of industrial relations, including an explanation for why the greater efficiencies of part-time labor are not already being exploited by profit-making enterprises.

Let me begin by introducing a set of analytical tools that were originally developed by William Stanley Jevons, a nineteenth-century British economist who pioneered the marginal revolution in neoclassical economics.[16] In particular, I want to adduce two of the best known and most widely accepted principles of economics that Jevons invoked: the law of the diminishing marginal utility of income on the one hand, and the law of the increasing marginal disutility of labor on the other.

For those unfamiliar with these terms, the law of the diminishing marginal utility of income refers to the fact that the first dollars a worker earns on a job are always more valuable to him (in terms of the happiness they will bring) than the dollars he earns later in the day or the week. This is but another way of saying that people value necessities more than luxuries.

The law of the increasing marginal disutility of labor by contrast refers to the fact that the first hours on a job are always less onerous than the hours that follow later on in the day or week. In other words, fatigue—mental as well as muscular—grows progressively worse over the course of one's time on the job. This is a phenomenon that anyone who has ever worked a long day will be familiar with.

Jevons's stroke of genius was to graph these two laws on a single piece of paper. The result was a diagram (see figure 4) in which the number of hours on the job is plotted on the horizontal axis and the corresponding utilities and disutilities of income and labor (which are felt in the form of pleasure and pain) are plotted on the vertical axis. The resulting Jevons diagram is the focus of everything I am about to say, so study it carefully.

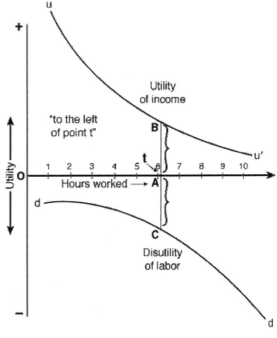

Figure 4

The first thing to note is that the upper curve representing the declining marginal utility of income lies entirely above the horizontal axis in the region of positive utility. It begins high on the left, indicating the high value a worker places on the first dollars he earns during his first hours on the job, after which it descends gradually downward along a curving path that approaches but never quite touches the horizontal axis where the utility of his wages would be zero. In the language of mathematics, we say this curve is *convex from below*.

The bottom curve, by contrast, which represents the increasing marginal disutility of labor, lies entirely below the horizontal axis in the region of negative utility. It too starts high on the left, this time signifying the relative ease of the first hours on a job, and bends ever more steeply downwards on a convex path that reflects the progressively intensifying physiological phenomenon known as fatigue. In the language of mathematics, it is *convex from above*.

I should point that neither of these "curves" is in fact a truly one-dimensional line, even though economists like to pretend that it is. It would have been less misleading on my part had I drawn them both using the side of a piece of chalk instead of the point. In any event, the only thing that really matters here is the general shape of the curves, not whether they can or cannot be accurately represented by a one-dimensional line. All we need to know is that the first curve is convex from above while the second is convex from below.

For much the same reason, readers will notice that the vertical axis representing positive and negative utility is not labeled in units, the reason being that science is incapable of measuring with any precision the purely subjective feelings of pleasure and pain we all experience.

Nonetheless, Jevons observed that there would always be a "point" (or rather a "fuzzy zone") t on the horizontal axis where the anticipated utility of the last dollar earned on the job would roughly counterbalance the actually experienced physical and mental discomfort required to earn those last additional dollars. He reasoned that any rational employee would voluntarily labor only up to that point (or zone) beyond which the disutility of his labor would begin to progressively exceed the anticipated utility of any additional money he would make. Put another way, the zone marked t was not only the zone of equilibrium between pleasure and pain; it was also the zone of maximum job satisfaction.

Suppose now that a worker, for whatever reason, is forced by his employer to continue working beyond point t after which the marginal disutility of his labor begins to exceed the marginal utility of his wages. How would that worker be inclined to react? His most natural inclination might be to slack off toward the end of day as a way to ease his growing fatigue. Or alternatively, he might show up late for work repeatedly as a way to simultaneously *increase* the marginal utility of his income (because his paycheck being smaller, the last dollars would be worth more) and *decrease* the marginal disutility of his labor (because his hours on the job would be fewer). Or alternatively, he might elect to not even come in to work on certain days of the week, which, even though it would leave the length of his workday unchanged, would reduce his paycheck at the end of the week and thereby increase the marginal utility of his wages. All three of these changes in behavior represent perfectly rational strategies for a worker to maximize his total job satisfaction.

WHAT PROFIT IT?

His employer, by contrast, would be most unhappy with any of them. His only recourse in all three cases would be the same, namely, to threaten to fire the worker if he doesn't straighten up. At that point the worker would be faced with a choice of either quitting, getting fired, or modifying his behavior at least partially to bring it more in line with his employer's demand. If he chooses the last of these three alternatives, no doubt because he feels that he cannot afford to quit or get fired, he would almost certainly develop a bad attitude on the job, which would betray his state of unhappiness. In extreme cases he might even resort to acts of vandalism or theft. Experienced employers will be familiar with all three of these possible changes in behavior since they are fundamental phenomena in the field of industrial relations.

I would now like to take the argument in a different direction, but in order to do so I need to first highlight three assumptions Jevons tacitly made when he developed this set of analytical tools. First, he assumed that the length of the workday and the number of workdays in the week were both fixed by custom—which of course they actually were at the time he was writing and indeed as they continue to be even today. Second, he tacitly assumed that the pace of work was also established by custom and was much the same for every employee doing the same job. This is also generally the case even now. And third, he assumed that the hourly wage rate was fixed beforehand by mutual agreement between each worker and his employer.

THE SEVENTH MILLENNIUM

Let us now see what happens if we relax these three assumptions either one at a time or in some combination.

First, suppose the customary hours of labor are reduced while the customary work pace and hourly wage rates remain unchanged. In that case, every employee by definition will be moved to the left on the horizontal axis on the Jevons diagram denoting the number of hours on the job. For some employees, like the dissatisfied worker I describe in the first example above, this will be a welcome change since it will move him closer to the point where he experiences maximum job satisfaction. Consequently, his rates of tardiness and absenteeism would be likely to decline or disappear altogether even as his attitude on the job would improve.

But what about the workers who were quite happy before? They would now be moved off of their point of maximum job satisfaction into the region where the utility of their wages exceeded the disutility of their labor. If given a choice they would now be more likely to quit their present employer and look for better opportunities elsewhere.

Let us now imagine a different scenario. What would happen should an employer inform each of his employees that while his hours on the job would remain the same, henceforth his hourly wage rate would change in proportion to any changes in his output per man-hour. Here again the response would vary depending on where each employee stood in relation to his own particular point t on the graph. Those who previously had more

40

hours than they wanted would slow their work pace even though they knew it would mean that their paychecks would be smaller. Those who were quite happy before on the other hand, would not change their behavior at all; they would continue working at the same pace in return for the same weekly paycheck they had been getting all along. Finally, what about those workers who had fewer hours on the job than they would have voluntarily preferred? They and they alone would be likely to work harder in an effort to increase the size of their paychecks.

As for the employer, his rate of return on investment could either go up, down, or remain the same depending on what fraction of his employees fell into in each of these categories.

I now want to look at the case with which we are actually concerned in this book. What would happen if, in addition to adjusting each employee's hourly wage rate in proportion to his output per man-hour, his hours of employment were cut in half even as he would henceforth be allowed to freely adjust his own pace of work? With that particular combination of changes, I contend that the response would depend almost entirely on the life situations of the various workers involved.

Consider first the situation of the typical working-class family with children today, assuming it resides in a large metropolitan area and that both parents are working a full forty-hour week. It seems highly unlikely that either parent would be able to increase his or her work pace to fully compensate for a fifty-percent reduction in hours

41

since that would imply a doubling (i.e., a one-hundred-percent increase) in their output per man-hour. Thus, their joint family income would almost certainly fall, which would put them at a distinct disadvantage when it comes to affording the one thing most parents want more than anything else: a nice house in a safe neighborhood with good public schools. They simply would not be able to compete for these scarce commodities with families in which both parents continue to work full-time. We may conclude, therefore, that a factory in a big city run on part-time jobs would not be able to recruit a workforce. And since most factories are in fact located in major metropolitan areas, this explains why we do not see many employers taking advantage of the greater efficiencies inherent in concept of incentive-base work sprints.

Families fortunate enough to live in one of our new country towns, on the other hand, would face an entirely different situation. Not only would they be able to afford the price of real estate in a good neighborhood composed of similarly situated families, but as I have already shown, it would be under circumstances that would allow them to make a much better use of their free time and limited resources than would be possible in a big city.

Perhaps the easiest way to understand the difference is by looking more closely at the distinction between necessities and luxuries. For working-class families who live in big cities the basic necessities are groceries, rent, utilities, and transportation. Luxuries are pretty much everything else. But for a family living in one of our new country towns this distinction is much harder to draw. You could almost say that necessities and luxuries had now been rolled into one and that both were contained in the new lifestyle itself—a lifestyle that by all historical standards would have to be considered the greatest luxury of all. In other words, the new way of life can best be understood as an all-or-nothing proposition, which means that the marginal utility of income of those engaged in it should remain very high, with all the desirable qualities that this would imply from an employer's point of view.

iv

It is time now to get down to brass tacks. Just how much faster and more efficiently might manufacturers expect such factories to run? In percentage terms, how big of an increase in output per man-hour are they likely to see?

This is of course the million-dollar question—and not just from the employer's point of view, but from the point of view of his employees as well, since both profits and wages are scheduled to go up together.

The fact is, however, that this is an empirical question that no amount of theory can even estimate. It is unfortunate, therefore, that very little good empirical data exists. Factories in the countryside employing nothing but a part-time workforce have never been tried. Nevertheless, in the course of my research over the years,

THE SEVENTH MILLENNIUM

I have been able to discover some empirical evidence that bears on the issue. And on the basis of this evidence, I think it is possible to form a rough estimate. I will now summarize what I have been able to find, including the results of a rather modest experiment that I myself conducted as a small-time employer.

The first and perhaps the most relevant piece of evidence I discovered involved a number of sorting sheds that were operated by UPS in the rural Midwest in the 1980s. UPS is of course a company well known for its high wages and the hustle of its employees. These particular sorting sheds were in rural areas outside of Chicago, and they were staffed mostly by women recruited from local farm families. Their job was to sort packages in the middle of the night for the next day's delivery. What was unusual in this particular case is that instead of paying each member of the crew a set hourly wage, UPS promised to pay the whole a group a set amount of money no matter how quickly or slowly they finished the job. With that understanding, UPS found that a crew could typically finish a job in three to four hours that used to take five or six hours when hourly wages were agreed to beforehand. I got this information in personal conversations with company officials back in the 1980s.

Around the same time, the economic historian Robert Heilbroner brought to my attention a privately held company in Cleveland, Ohio, that had hit upon the idea of combining incentive pay with a (somewhat)

44

shorter workweek. This was The Lincoln Electric Company, a manufacturer of welding equipment whose founder, James Lincoln, had put in place a radical profit-sharing plan in conjunction with a flexible work-sharing arrangement that varied the hours of his employees depending on the ups and downs in demand for his arc welding equipment.[17]

And a few years later, I was able to identify another company, Steelcase Inc., a manufacturer of office furnishings that also combined profit sharing with work sharing in a similar fashion. Based on news reports, Lincoln Electric and Steelcase were both significantly more profitable than their competitors, paying wages and generating a return on investment twenty to forty percent above the industry average. Furthermore, both companies dominated the industries they were in.

These results are consistent with my own experience as a small-time employer. For a quarter of a century, my wife and I owned and operated a small landscape-gardening company in southeast Tennessee, where we spent most of our time installing "gardens for rich people," as I used to say. My wife was the garden designer and horticulturalist while I ran the crews. For the first three years, we hired common laborers—country boys, mostly, from the back of Signal Mountain—whom we paid by the hour just like all of our competitors were doing. We worked a six-hour day and a four-day week on average owing to inclement weather and the seasonal nature of our business. In other words, a twenty-four-hour week was the norm.

In 1981, a year and a half after my letter to the Fantus Company I decided it was time to put my pet theory to the test. My wife was reluctant to go along until I convinced her that we really had nothing to lose. This was because I planned to offer our employees the same share of our proceeds that they had been getting all along.

So it was that one day, having just finished a job, I sat down with my crew on the ground with job sheets in hand and went over in great detail the last dozen installations that we had completed together. On the front side of each job sheet was a carbon copy of the actual contract signed by the customer that listed all the plants, topsoil, stone, mulches, and other materials that we had contracted to install along with the total price of the job that the customer had agreed to pay. On the back of each sheet was a list of the wholesale prices I had actually paid for these materials, to which I had stapled all the supporting wholesale receipts. Finally, at the bottom of each sheet was a record of the hours each worker had worked on that job and his hourly wage rate.

With this information in hand, it was a simple matter to calculate what I called the *net product* on each job, which was defined quite simply as the contract price minus the total cost of materials. (*Value added* is another term for the same thing.) Next, I calculated the size of the total wage bill expressed as a percentage of the net product. Based on the last dozen jobs, these wage bills

46

were averaging twenty-nine percent of the average net product. This was a simple historical fact. Furthermore, once the size of the wage bill for each job had been calculated, it was easy to compute each worker's share of that bill based on the number of hours he had worked on the job times his hourly wage rate.

Having explained all this to my crew in great detail, I then asked them what they thought of the idea that on future jobs, I simply pay them as a group that same twenty-nine percent of the net product they had been getting all along, which would then be divided among them based on how many hours each member of the crew had worked on that particular installation times his nominal wage rate. If I paid them that way, I carefully explained, if they were able to complete a job more quickly (with fewer man-hours) than in the past, they would still get the same total amount of pay even though they earned it over a shorter period of time. Seeing the logic of my proposal, including the possibility of increasing the size of their paychecks at the end of each week if they completed more jobs, they agreed to give my proposal a try.

What happened next was a roughly forty-percent increase in average output per man-hour—an increase that started on the very next job and remained more or less constant throughout the rest of that planting season and over the course of the next twenty years.

The key to this success, I am convinced, lay in my decision to share with my employees three key pieces of

47

information that most employers keep secret: the contract price of the job, the wholesale cost of the materials, and each worker's nominal hourly wage rate (including my own, which was considerably higher than theirs, I should mention). Total transparency together with my practice of computing the net product and each worker's share of it at the end of each job, typically while sitting under a tree in the customer's yard with my crew gathered around and a pile of wholesale receipts lying on the ground—these were the magic ingredients that made the plan work. For there were no secrets here and everybody knew it. And believe me when I say that whenever I made a mistake in my arithmetic, which happened sometimes even though I was using a calculator, the members of the crew were not slow about pointing it out. In other words, so long as they felt they could trust me and that I wasn't trying to put one over on them, my workers were completely on board with this new arrangement.

And, indeed, why shouldn't they have been on board? They were now taking home on average forty percent more at the end of each week than they had in the past, which was forty percent more than a lot of their friends who worked for my competitors were making.

And since we could get more work done in a shorter period of time, our company's annual rate of profit also increased forty percent, which of course was the whole point of the exercise. Plus, I discovered a number of fringe benefits I had not fully anticipated. For one thing, it didn't seem to matter anymore whether I was on the jobsite or not. I no longer had to keep a sharp eye on my employees to make sure they were actually working and not resting on their shovels, something I had always hated doing anyway. Furthermore, if I hired a new worker (our little company was growing) and he started goofing off on the job the first time I was away, his co-workers lost no time putting him in his place. They were all working for each other now, as they soon came to realize, and they made damn sure that every new employee knew that as well.

I also noticed less waste of time and materials. There were fewer damaged root balls and broken limbs, fewer poorly planted trees and shrubs that would have to be replanted. My plantsmen (they were no longer common laborers, at least in my eyes) were now paying closer attention to the finer points of landscape design: to the shaping of the beds, the spacing of the plants, the drawing of the borders, etc. In short, I was seeing less of everything that might get them fired or reduce the size of their paychecks. Which isn't to say there weren't issues of quality control that I still had to monitor. Making sure that my workers were properly amending the soil with the right amount of peat moss and that they weren't skimping on mulches are the two that I remember best. But all in all, I was gratified to learn that henceforth I had been relieved of many of the burdens of managing a crew, which of course the crew liked because it meant I spent less time on the job, and which minimized my share of the wage bill based on my hourly wage rate (which I had deliberately set considerably higher than theirs).

My wife would occasionally wonder why we were paying our employees so much more by the week than our competitors did. She would especially complain whenever she landed a particularly fat job with high profit margins. On those occasions, I could only say in my defense that the more money they were making, the more we were making too. Plus, I pointed out that whenever she underbid a job our employees weren't slow in letting us know; that kind of instant feedback was worth something, too. I also pointed out that we no longer suffered many of the headaches that were endemic to our trade. Chronic absenteeism and high turnover were no longer issues, nor did we have to worry about losing our best workers to other landscape companies in the area. These were problems that plagued our industry, causing not a few of our competitors to quit the field altogether.

v

I now want to describe the kinds of factories that are best suited to incentive-based work sprints, but before I get into that complicated subject, let me say something about the future of manufacturing in America more generally. Indeed, does manufacturing even have a future in United States?

WHAT PROFIT IT?

Many pundits have been writing for quite some time that it doesn't have a future. They point to a never-ending stream of new labor-saving technologies that are constantly being introduced onto America's factory floors and to the relocation of many labor-intensive forms of manufacture to low-wage countries in Asia and Latin America. As a consequence, they note that manufacturing employment in the United States has been steadily declining from roughly thirty percent of the workforce half a century ago to less than twelve percent today. We are entering a new "post-industrial age" they argue, one in which the overwhelming majority of ordinary working people won't be employed in factories but rather in a rapidly expanding service economy.[18]

This is all true, and there is little doubt that it will remain true so long as American workers continue to live in big cities and continue to work forty hours a week or longer. On the other hand, I should point out that under the terms of the new arrangement that I am proposing, a quite opposite conclusion can be reached. For one thing, it is quite clear that working families will no longer be living in a service economy to the extent that they go back to doing things for themselves and each other that they currently pay other people to do for them. To the extent that happens, the service economy's share of total employment will go down, most dramatically of course in the new towns themselves. Equally important, the percentage of the workforce engaged in manufacture will automatically double (from twelve percent to twenty-four

51

percent) simply by virtue of the fact that factories will now be employing roughly twice as many workers as before.

But there is an additional reason to be optimistic about the future of manufacturing in America. When Congress changed this country's trade laws at the end of the Cold War, it virtually forced many thousands of American manufacturers, especially those in relatively low-skill, labor-intensive industries, to relocate to low-wage countries overseas if they intended to stay in business in a competitive world.[19] The results are plain to see all across rust-belt America. But now that the human costs have become too glaring to ignore, there are signs that the era of low tariffs and free mobility of capital may be about to end and that a new era of protectionism may be about to begin. If that indeed happens, it will force many of those very same manufacturers who went abroad to return to these shores if they intend to make things to sell in this country, which, lest anyone forgets, remains one of the three biggest markets in the world. That would entail thousands of new factories being built here in the United States, many of which would be well suited to incentive-based work sprints should they locate in rural areas.

But even leaving that possibility aside, and without trying to downplay or minimize the impact of automation and outsourcing over the past several decades, it is important to realize that manufacturing remains the single biggest source of employment in America. There are roughly 250,000 small- and medium-sized manufacturers (defined as those with five hundred employees or fewer but with a median number of fifty) who continue to do business in the United States today. [20] These are manufacturers I want to focus on here. Which among them would be best suited to incentive-based work sprints?

vi

To answer that question, it will be useful to distinguish between the short and the long run. That is to say, we need to distinguish between those manufacturing processes that could benefit immediately—for which only minor changes in their existing processes of production would be needed—and those that would require major reengineering and new capital inputs. Since the ones that could benefit right away are the simplest to deal with, I will look at them first.

Simplest of all are factories that pay by the piece. This is because under a piece-rate system, any increase in average output per man-hour translates automatically into an identical percentage increase in both the average hourly wage rate and the rate of return on investment (notwithstanding the fact that unit-labor costs would not change at all). Or to put it another way, as long as economies of scale are maintained, a smaller outlay for plant and equipment would support the same total output, which also translates into a higher rate of return on investment. That being said, we should note that piece rates are not nearly as common as they once were, the garment industry in particular having largely migrated overseas.

Let me now pass on to the second simplest category. These would be factories whose operations require the cooperation of a number of employees working in concert but whose output can vary depending on the collective intensity of their efforts. This was the case with my own small landscaping company as I described it above. It was also the case with those rural sorting sheds that were operated by UPS. It was likely the case with the Lincoln Electric Co. and Steelcase Inc., though here I have no inside information. Indeed, it is usually, if not always, the case with traditional assembly-line production processes. It was certainly the case in one small factory I worked in one summer in Berkeley, California, where a group of five people assembled vacuum pumps for high school science laboratories. It was partly the case in another much larger factory I once worked in—this one in Germany in 1962—that manufactured high-precision drill chucks. I will have more to say about that particular factory in a moment. Finally, it is sometimes the case with companies that manufacture machinery or machine parts, including machine tools, and other large pieces of industrial equipment, whether one of a kind or in small production runs. This is a category of industry that is thriving in the United States today and that seems likely to continue thriving for decades to come, exporting much of its product to customers overseas.

The same logic applies to this second category as applied to manufacturers who pay by the piece. In both kinds of factories, even though unit-labor costs remain unchanged, greater efforts on the part of labor can result in increases in output per man-hour, which can then be divided between capital and labor in a way that results in the same percentage of increase in hourly wage rates and the rate of return on investment. There is little doubt that a significant fraction of the 250,000 small- and medium-size manufacturers doing business today will fall into this second category.

A third category is composed of manufacturing operations whose rate of output cannot be made to vary in the short run without redesigning the machinery, but in which the number of employees required to operate the machinery can vary depending on how hard they work. Textile and carpet mills fall into this category, as do most other forms of machine tending. A single operator might be able to tend any number of pieces of equipment depending on how quickly he moves. The difficulty in these types of situations lies in the fact that increases in output per man-hour do not translate into changes in the rate of output of the facility as a whole. Thus, a more complex formula is required in order to share the gains in productivity equally between labor and capital. I will come back to this problem in a moment.

But first, I want to highlight a second limitation in these types of situations. Increases in labor productivity, no matter how dramatic, will be insignificant from the employer's point of view unless the number of workers employed in a facility is large relative to the amount of capital invested in plant and equipment. To see why this is so, let us take an extreme example: an oil refinery, say, or even better, a nuclear power plant manned by a small handful of workers. In both cases, it should be obvious that the total wage bill will be an insignificant fraction of the total costs of production. Thus, changes in labor productivity will be equally insignificant. This is why at the outset I stipulated that the argument in favor of incentive-based work sprints would only apply to facilities that employ significant quantities of both labor and capital.

vii

Let me now turn from the relatively simple categories of production to the much more complex situations typically found in most factories today, starting with those that involve a mixture of categories. This was the case in that German factory I worked in making drill chucks. Some of the steps in the process of production—including the milling machine that I operated, polishing the surface of a certain metal part—could easily have been paid by the piece. This was owing to the fact that the

56

rate of output was based entirely on the skill of the operator. Other steps in production were strictly a function of the engineered speed of the various milling machines employed, some of which required a set number of operators no matter how hard they worked. There were yet other steps of production in which the number of operators could vary depending on their effort either singly or in groups.

Or take the case of a piece of machinery that has been engineered to operate at a certain customary speed, but which could be extensively reengineered to take advantage of a more highly motivated workforce. This is not an uncommon situation. In fact, whole assembly lines are sometimes engineered to run at a speed that has been negotiated beforehand in accordance to the demands of organized labor.

Then there is the fundamental reality that all machinery wears out with use and must be replaced from time to time. New machinery may cost more than the old, which means new capital expenditures will be required just to keep a factory running. This raises the vexing issue of how to evaluate the total amount of capital invested in a factory at a particular moment in time, something that must be done in order to equitably share improvements in productivity between labor and capital.

But this is only a special case of a far more general reality. Machinery not only wears out, but it becomes obsolete over time. New and improved versions of capital equipment, including new labor-saving technologies, appear on the market with regularity, which firms in many cases must employ in order to compete. New products begin to be produced using existing or newly modernized facilities even as the old ones fade away or are abandoned or completely redesigned. To say nothing of the fact that throughout the economy and across every industry, the relative demand for labor and capital is continually in flux.

In a static world, such as with my small landscaping company, historical data forms the ideal basis for deriving a formula to divide the net product between labor and capital. But it proves to be a poor guide over the long term in the ever-changing world we actually live in—a world in which labor and management must forever be negotiating and then renegotiating the contract that both divides them and binds them together.

It would be wonderful of course if we could identify a set of empirical parameters out there in the world that could be objectively measured with a tolerable degree of precision, on the basis of which contracts between labor and management could be negotiated. It was in search of such parameters that I once wrote a short academic paper, "A Note on Wages and Prices," that I have taken the liberty of appending to these notes. Truthfully, I no longer have the wit to tell whether this paper actually solves the problem it sets out to solve or whether it even fully makes sense. But I can say this much for it: that when I sent the first part to Milton Friedman at the University of Chicago in the summer of 1974, he wrote back saying that "for a professional carpenter," which I was at the time, I was "an excellent amateur economist" and that he hoped I would continue my research. At that moment on my life's chosen path, I needed those words of encouragement. He was a very generous man.

Years later I might add we corresponded again, only this time at great length, over a long article that *Harper's Magazine* had commissioned me to write on the subject of free trade and its likely consequences for the future of American society, about which we politely disagreed. See Appendix IV for the substance of our disagreement.

Chapter Three
A Business Plan

For which of you, intending to build a tower, sitteth not down first and counteth the cost, whether he hath sufficient to finish it.[21]

In this chapter, I shall explore the physical and the financial challenge of building a new town from scratch. And not just any new town, of course, but one that adheres to the principles of a true garden city and whose economy will be anchored by factories of the new type that are at the heart of this book.

The first thing that needs to be said is that building a new town from scratch is a difficult and exceedingly complex undertaking even in the best of circumstances, let alone when subject to these additional criteria. It will involve a carefully coordinated coming together of large amounts of labor and capital in a place that, by assumption, is economically undeveloped and therefore largely lacking in infrastructure.

If we hope to succeed in such an undertaking, we need to be realistic from the outset. This will not be a job for amateurs. To pull it off is going to require the combined efforts of a wide range of specialized talents and proven abilities such as only a small army of experienced professionals can possibly supply. The list will include real estate developers, urban planners, landscape architects, civil engineers, project managers, building contractors, corporate farmers, industrial recruiters, business consultants, lawyers, lobbyists, politicians, journeymen in all the major building trades, and last but not least, financial experts of every description. Qualified individuals in all of these fields will have to be enlisted to the cause, in the vast majority of cases as fully compensated professionals. I will have more to say on how we might go about finding and paying for all this talent in the following chapter. But in this chapter, I want to highlight the physical dimensions of the problem that this body of talent will be called upon to solve.

ii

The reader will recall from chapter one the initial sequence of steps by which an organized group might go about building a new garden city from scratch. Let us therefore assume that a suitable town site has already been located and that the purchase has been completed using conventional financing (about which I shall have more to say in due course). I shall also assume that a new municipality has been legally incorporated whose boundaries completely encompass the site, and that a broad set of plans has been drawn up by a group of professional town planners in a manner that fits the topographical features of the particular site chosen.

The issue now becomes, How best to proceed? Should we try to build the town to completion in the shortest time possible? Or would it be better to proceed slowly, in a more cautious manner?

If the aim is to maximize our chances of success, then I would like to argue in favor of the second of these two options. In particular, I want to show just why it would be wiser to build the town very gradually and in stages, taking care to be guided every step of the way by a new precautionary principle that I shall dub the *rule of new austerity*.

Let me now explain what I mean by this rule of austerity and why I believe it is likely to prove so vitally important

The easiest way to do this is to imagine what might happen were we to try to build the new town to completion in the shortest time possible. Using available data it is possible to estimate the total amount of money that would have to be spent in order to build a new town from scratch for a population of twenty-five thousand. That is, we can estimate how much it would cost to install all the necessary infrastructure—roads, bridges, gas and water mains, electrical and communication grids, sewage and storm drainage systems, and the like—to which we must add the cost of building all the schools, parks, playgrounds, fire halls, police stations, churches, medical facilities, government office buildings, and the various kinds of stores and other commercial establishments that are typical for a town of that size. The total would be in the neighborhood of half a billion dollars, unless I am greatly mistaken.[22]

But this is only half of the story. To this total we must add the costs of building and equipping all the factories on which the community will depend for its economic independence, plus all the building materials, furniture, household appliances, and the like that would go into eight thousand residential structures (assuming two structures for each of four thousand extended families of six), to say nothing of the money that will be needed to feed and support the people who will be building these structures before the factories open their doors.

The grand total would now be in the neighborhood of a billion dollars, most of which would have to be borrowed from private lending institutions. What is more, when we take into account the high risks involved in such a novel undertaking, we must assume that the rates of interest charged on these loans will be substantially higher than for more conventional building projects and that the institutions making these loans will insist upon holding all the town's assets as collateral in case of default.

The critical question can now be stated quite clearly: How much time will elapse between when the loans are extended and the time when they can begin to be paid off? In other words, how long before the town is fully up and running, at which point it will start generating income, a portion of which can be used to start paying down its

64

debts? Even assuming that everything goes smoothly and according to plan, it will likely be a matter of years, during which time the interest on the loans will mount exponentially.

But now let us suppose that everything doesn't go smoothly and according to plan. What happens if there is an unanticipated downturn in the economy that causes the bankers to get cold feet? Or if there is a sudden bout of inflation and long-term interest rates spike up dramatically? Or if due to changing market conditions, some of the expected factories fail to materialize?

Unless I am greatly mistaken, were one or more of these far-from-uncommon events to occur, the town could easily find itself in a situation in which its total indebtedness clearly exceeded its future capacity to pay. And were that to happen, the town and many of its residents would eventually find themselves falling into bankruptcy, one of the consequences of which is that they could then be forced to sell off their assets. By assumption, these assets would include all the town's commercial real estate and all of the potentially quite developable acreage in the surrounding greenbelt. At which point it would be good-bye garden city, hello urban sprawl.

THE SEVENTH MILLENNIUM

iii

To avoid such a calamity, the wiser course is to build the town only gradually and in stages in accordance with the rule of austerity. I will now try to picture what following that scenario might look like.

We can begin with the site of the future garden city itself, which, by assumption, will exist in an economically undeveloped state. Since we have already stipulated that this site will consist of productive farmland purchased at fair market value, we can assume that with proper management it should be able to generate enough income to cover the interest on the loan used to purchase it over an indefinite period of time. (I will have more to say on how to finance the initial land purchase in the following chapter.) It follows that farming and the processing of agricultural products will be the first sources of permanent employment for the town's first wave of settlers. Their job will be to profitably utilize every acre of farmland right up until the moment it is finally converted to nonagricultural uses.

Let us now imagine that a visitor has come to see just what is going on at the site of one of these future new towns shortly after first construction begins. After inspecting the farming operations, which he notices occupy almost of the entire site, he walks to the area where the future downtown commercial district is scheduled to be built. Of course there will be nothing there that resembles a traditional courthouse square cum galleria just yet. Instead, he will see something that looks more like a mining camp in an old Hollywood Western, complete with a general store on a dusty street and, next to it, a primitive hotel with a bar and grill on the ground floor that serves as the center of the camp's social life. If there are many women or children about, which seems more than likely since the men will have wives, he might see a one-room schoolhouse that doubles as a church on Sundays. Most definitely there will be a large lumberyard and an unsightly cement plant in full public view, around which will be scattered an assortment of heavy equipment such as one commonly encounters on any large construction site: graders, dozers, loaders, excavators, backhoes, trenchers, dump trucks, etc. A little farther off in the distance will be a large open field that is dotted with campers and tents. This is where the construction workers representing all the major building trades will be housed temporarily. Their job will be to gradually build out the town's infrastructure and to erect, but only as needed, all of the nonresidential structures in the town, including the factories. These construction workers, in other words, along with their wives and children, will constitute the town's second group of permanent residents.

If our hypothetical visitor should venture out a little further from the town center, he might come upon the site of a future neighborhood community where the local infrastructure is just being installed. And if he keeps walking, he will encounter a nearby industrial park where the first factory is already starting to go up. At this point, he will realize something important: that residential districts and industrial parks are being developed in tandem, one neighborhood and one factory at a time, care being taken to keep the number of new settlers closely in line with their opportunities for employment. I'll have more to say on how future neighborhood groups will be recruited and matched with their future employers in the next chapter.

iv

Let us now imagine that our visitor wanders back to the site of that first neighborhood that was just beginning to be graded, to watch how it gradually takes shape. Of course it will never look anything like one of those brand spanking new subdivisions that spring up like mushrooms in the exurbs of our big cities today. First movers-in will be met with no gated entranceways, no paved roads, no sidewalks, and no streetlights, not even a fully functioning sewage system. This isn't to say there won't be any preliminary development whatsoever. As already stipulated, the plans for the new town will already have been drawn up, including the exact location and layout of each future neighborhood unit right down to the individual lot lines. Moreover, as I just indicated, the neighborhood's basic infrastructure will have been installed, if only a few days before its future families are scheduled to begin arriving on the scene. They will be relieved to learn that not only have the streets and back alleyways been graded and graveled, but that the various underground utilities have been stubbed in right up to the lot lines.

As for the future neighborhood green, it will be little more than an open field with perhaps a few saplings planted around the perimeter. There won't be any swing sets, basketball courts, horseshoe pits, or park benches, let alone a covered pavilion or neighborhood clubhouse. Amenities like these will one day appear, but not until all the families in the neighborhood decide that they can collectively afford to build them.

v

I come now to the subject of house building itself—or, to be more precise, to the notion of the families in a neighborhood building their own houses—that is central to the new way of life described in these pages. I will begin with a preliminary question, namely, Is it realistic to assume that ordinary people will be able to build their own houses? As a matter of fact this is the very first question I asked myself when the idea of part-time jobs in the country and how we might get them in numbers first entered my mind—which happened, incidentally, in the course of an interview that I, a self-described amateur anthropologist at the time, was conducting with a young

69

hippie boy on a sidewalk in the Haight-Ashbury district of San Francisco in the spring of 1967. Like so many other hippies in the Haight during that extraordinary year, he had grown up in a suburban middle-class home and, as a consequence, was now disillusioned with that 1950s version of the American dream that his parents had worked so hard to achieve. Never mind why this was so. It was simply a fact. And like so many others, he too was now possessed by an intense desire to leave the big cities behind and go back to the land, where he envisioned himself leading a simple life that would include building his own house, with little thought being given to how he might support himself there. It was a highly attractive idea, even to me, but I was immediately aware of some of the practical issues involved, including whether people like him would in fact be capable of building their own houses. Having just graduated from a small liberal arts college a few months before, I knew absolutely nothing about how houses were built, including the necessary skills that would have to be mastered. So to find out, I arranged (with the help of my father, I should mention) to be accepted into the membership of the United Brotherhood of Carpenters in Marin County, California, where I entered what turned out to be an excellent apprenticeship training program.

What I learned over the course of the next year and a half is that it would indeed be possible for ordinary people to build their own houses, but that in order to do so they were going to require a certain amount of professional assistance. This would be especially true in the earliest phases of construction, which, I soon discovered, were not only the heaviest but also the most critical. Included here would be the initial layout of the building lines on the ground, the digging and pouring of the footings, and any block work or concrete form construction required to bring the foundations up to grade. If there were concrete floors to be poured and finished, professional guidance would be needed there as well.

And so it was that I eventually came to the realization that some of those same building tradesmen we encountered earlier in this chapter, the ones who were installing the town's infrastructure and erecting its nonresidential buildings, would have to be charged with the additional responsibility of assisting future families in precisely these ways.

vi

Let me now say something about housing costs, which are far and away the single biggest item in most families' budgets, consuming on average between thirty and thirty-five percent of their disposable incomes. In light of this fact, it will be useful to calculate the amount of money a family might save by building its own house, assuming it does so gradually and in stages over a period of time rather than all at one go, which it won't have the leisure to do in any event.

THE SEVENTH MILLENNIUM

The most obvious place to begin is with the expected savings in the cost of labor, which normally accounts for roughly forty percent of the cost of constructing a new house (with the other sixty percent going to the cost of materials).[23] Professional building tradesmen will still be on the job part of the time as we just saw, but primarily in a teaching role. The lion's share of the actual physical work will be done by the families themselves, assuming they are reasonably fit and take well to instruction. Assuming a three-quarters reduction in the amount of paid labor employed, which seems reasonable based on my first-hand experience, I expect we should see an immediate thirty-percent reduction in the total cost of construction (since three-quarters of forty percent equals thirty percent).

The next most obvious thing to consider is the low cost of the land on which the new house will be built, since, as the reader will recall, the cheapness of land in rural areas is one of the biggest motivating factors behind the whole garden city concept. Even good cropland goes for less than $5000 an acre on average in most parts of the United States nowadays. Pastureland goes for less than half of that. Building lots in residential neighborhoods in our major cities on the other hand typically cost ten, twenty, or even thirty times that amount per acre, which explains why the cost of the land now generally accounts for between a third and half of the cost of the house in big cities today. To take a concrete example, a house that costs $100,000 to build in labor and materials might cost

A BUSINESS PLAN

$150,000 to purchase (or even more if it is located in a safe neighborhood with good public schools) in one of our major metropolitan areas. By contrast, a family settling in one of our new neighborhood communities should be able to purchase a lot of equal or greater size and build an otherwise identical house for roughly half that amount (or $75,000) if we take into account the reductions in the costs of the labor as well as the land.

Finally, there are the costs of financing the purchase of a house that we need to consider. People who live and work in big cites today are rarely in a position to build their own houses, having neither the leisure nor the spare cash to do so. Instead, they are forced to purchase a house that has already been built by borrowing money from a bank, paying off the loan with interest over a period of years. Those interest payments, when you add them all up, turn out to be a major fraction of the total cost of owning a home. For instance, if we assume a four-percent mortgage rate, which is quite typical, then the total interest payments on a thirty-year mortgage sum to slightly more than seventy percent of the original amount borrowed. Thus (to continue the concrete example in the paragraph above), a house that cost $100,000 to build and $150,000 to purchase would end up costing the family more than $250,000 by the time it is completely paid off.

Every penny of this interest can be avoided by families who build their own houses, provided only that they save up ahead of time—or, rather, as they go along— the money needed to purchase the building materials they will require to continue each phase of construction. Admittedly, this means families will have to wait a number of years, perhaps ten or twelve, before their dream home is finally finished, and conditions are liable to be cramped in the meantime. But here again, as with the town as a whole, prudence favors those who proceed gradually and with a minimum of debt, thereby maximizing their long-term chances of success. Saving, not borrowing, must become the new order of the day.

Incidentally, this is why I propose in the next chapter that married couples not become eligible for resettlement until they have managed to set aside enough money to purchase a lot and enough building materials to get some kind of roof over their heads, no matter how primitive.

vii

So far I have said nothing about the cost of food. which, after housing and transportation, is the third biggest item in most families' budgets, making it a topic too important to be overlooked.

There are two related questions that need to be answered. First, how much money might a working-class family save by cooking and eating at home instead of eating out in fast food restaurants, as so many do today? And second, how much money might it save by growing

74

some of its fruits and vegetables at home instead of purchasing them in grocery stores.

According to research done by the U.S. Department of Agriculture, eating out in fast food restaurants is roughly twice as expensive as eating frozen meals at home, while frozen meals are roughly one and a half times as expensive as meals prepared from scratch using raw ingredients. Thus we can see that a working-class family might reduce its total spending on food by as much as one half when we consider the current eating habits of the average two-earner household living in a major metropolitan areas today.

What about the cost of fruits and vegetables grown at home versus those purchased in grocery stores? Here I think the evidence shows that the potential savings are really quite modest, particularly when one takes into account the amount of labor involved. Rather than money saved it is the issue of *quality* that really stands out here. It is a rare individual who doesn't prefer the taste of homegrown tomatoes or of sweet corn fresh off the stalk when compared to what one usually finds on supermarket shelves. Much the same can be said for fresh poultry, eggs, butter, cream, baby carrots, green beans, asparagus, strawberries, and any number of other fruits and vegetables that can be grown in a garden. It is not easy to put a price tag on luxuries such as these—except in the fanciest of restaurants, to be sure, where they fetch very high prices indeed.

THE SEVENTH MILLENNIUM

Then there are the simple pleasures of gardening itself, which Nathaniel Hawthorne once described in far better prose than I could ever hope to produce:

> *Not that it can be disputed, that the light toil, requisite to cultivate a moderately sized garden, imparts such zest to kitchen vegetables as is never found in those of the market gardener. Childless men, if they would know something of the bliss of paternity, should plant a seed,—be it squash, bean, Indian corn, or perhaps a mere flower or worthless weed,—should plant it with their own hands, and nurse it from infancy to maturity altogether by their own care. If there not be too many of them, each individual plant becomes an object of separate interest. My garden, that skirted the avenue of the Manse, was of precisely the right extent. An hour or two of morning labor was all that it required. But I used to visit it and revisit it a dozen times a day, and stand in deep contemplation of my vegetable progeny . . . .*[24]

And as with food and the simple pleasures of gardening, so it is with many of the other areas of life that we have been exploring in these pages: the satisfactions that come with building one's house in the company of people you love; the liberty and leisure of the unencumbered individual; a new, more partnered relationship between labor and capital; improvements in the quality of childcare and of life in old age; the benefits of living in a true neighborhood community composed of like-minded families; and, last but not least, a revitalization of the civic life and political institutions of the new towns themselves, in which the American ideal of local self-government might reach its fullest possible expression. In every instance issues of quality make it impossible to estimate what the new standard of living will be as compared to the way we live now. It would certainly be a mistake to make average family income by itself standard of measure, though even by that standard the results might be surprising. But in this case I think even academic economists will agree that there is only one valid way to compare two very different ways of life. We must appeal to what in the jargon of the profession is known as *revealed preference*. In other words, Which of the two alternatives will people prefer if given a free choice in the matter?

viii

But of course it is one thing to tell a pollster how interested one would be in a hypothetically described new way of living, and quite another when faced with the realities and challenges that might actually be involved. So let me conclude this chapter by returning to the rule of austerity, only this time considered not as a matter of prudence but rather as a value in and of itself. What interests me is the power of austerity to foster a strong sense of community among those who practice it, upon which the long-term survival of our new towns is likely to depend.

What is a community, after all? The classic sociological definition is "a group of people who feel that they belong together."[25] Traditionally such feelings of belongingness were the product of many generations, nurtured by networks of families marrying, living, and dying together. Those kinds of communities have largely disappeared in the West, however. They were swept away in that maelstrom of progress known as the Industrial Revolution, which was so vividly described by Engels and Marx in their *Communist Manifesto*.

For well over a century now, the only real communities to be found in the United States—or, rather, the only communities of any real permanence—have been composed of families welded together by a common purpose and a shared vision of the future. The Mormons and Amish furnish two of the best-known examples, and it is no coincidence that in both cases we are talking about religious communities. Nor is it an accident that the religious glue holding them together places strenuous physical as well as moral demands upon their adherents, if only to separate the wheat from the chaff.[26]

From this we may conclude that the Big Rock Candy Mountain should never be mistaken for Zion. It is time to admit that the new way of life I am proposing in

A BUSINESS PLAN

these pages will not be an easy one, at least not in the beginning. Great sacrifices are going to be required along the way. It won't be for everyone, that much is for sure. Which is but another way of saying something that Jesus said a long time ago: that there will be—there must be—a great sorting out.

Chapter Four
The Corporate Imperative

So we, being many, are one body in Christ, and every one members one of another.[27]

incorporate, v. (from the Latin *corpore,* "to unite in one body"), to form into a body distinct from the state and endowed by law with the rights and responsibilities of a person; adj., united in one body.

corporation, n. (from the Latin *corporatio,* "united in one body"), a body of associated individuals with its own legal rights and responsibilities and with the capacity of succession.

The private corporation is one of the distinguishing institutions of modern Western civilization.[28] Together with the rule of law, individual rights, private enterprise, republican forms of government, and the prohibition of consanguineous and polygamous forms of marriage,[29] it is one of the building blocks that set our civilization apart from the many archaic, not to say barbarous forms of civilization that have existed in the past—and that in fact continue to exist in many parts of the world even to this day, including, most notably, in communist China, but also throughout much of Southwest Asia, Africa, and

Latin America. To appreciate the importance of private corporations as legal institutions, one need only recall the many roles they have played in the history of the West since medieval times: as churches, monasteries, chartered towns, craft and merchant guilds, banks, universities, hospitals, trading companies, colonial enterprises, charitable foundations, scientific societies, political parties, labor unions, civic organizations, and last but not least in the form of the modern joint-stock limited liability business corporation.

Indeed, it is quite impossible to imagine a truly civilized society without private corporations since it is the rise to power of these non-state actors that makes our civilization "civil" in the first place. Contrast this to the situation in China today, where there are no private institutions of any kind— including the family itself!— that are free from the arbitrary will of a Leninist one-party state, and where the very phrase *civil society* has been banned from all public discourse.

The legendary union organizer John L. Lewis once put the case for corporations (in his case, a labor union) quite eloquently in some words he addressed a group of coal miners in eastern Kentucky. "Unorganized," he said, "you are a lone individual, invisible, unrecognized, without influence of any kind. But from the moment you are accepted into the membership of a true corporation you have the aid of your fellow man."

With that thought in mind, let us contemplate the possibility of chartering a wholly new kind of corporation here in the United States: one that is Hebraic in spirit and in its religious orientation, yet with a clearly defined secular goal, namely, to promote the new way of life proposed in these pages. This new type of corporation will need to be in the form of a dues-paying national membership organization and it must be open to all Americans who aspire to the new way of life "without regard to race, creed, color, or country of origin." Furthermore it must be nonsectarian, by which I mean there must be no religious test for membership beyond a simple pledge of loyalty to the organization's clearly stated secular goal *"as it can be understood in the Judeo-Christian tradition upon which our civilization was founded."*[30] Understanding, not belief, in other words, should be the only thing required.

But before I go any further, let me pause to admit that in practical matters of organization I have very little first-hand experience and, based on that experience, even less talent. I know for a surety that there are men and women all over this land who are far better qualified than I am to pronounce on these matters. If we are going to succeed in our mission it is essential that these individuals be identified and that their ideas and proposals be carefully considered. Let us therefore pledge to ourselves and each other to let reason and common sense alone— not appeals to authority, not personal charisma, and least of all not dazzling displays of intellectual brilliance which serve only to blind us even as they fail to illuminate[31]—be our only guides.

THE SEVENTH MILLENNIUM

That being said, I would now like to state my general views on the subject for what they are worth.

ii

My first and most considered view is that the new organization ought to model itself on the only other organization in modern times that had a similar objective and was faced with a similar set of obstacles. I refer to the World Zionist Organization (WZO), which over a period of decades in the first half of the twentieth century organized the resettlement of a select portion of European Jewry in an economically undeveloped region of Palestine.[32] Like the new organization I am contemplating here, the WZO was at heart a colonizing venture. It, too, had a secular mission yet was motivated by a millennial ideal. And it, too, faced the manifold challenge of identifying, recruiting, training, and assisting large numbers of (for the most part) idealistic young people to build new lives for themselves in a place that was far from the places of their birth.

But of course there are important differences too, the most obvious one being that the WZO was international in scope, having committed itself to the seemingly utopian task of assisting the members of a persecuted and largely impoverished religious minority residing in a dozen different European countries, few of them liberal democracies, to emigrate to a brand new

84

political state that it was simultaneously attempting to organize in a hostile corner of the Ottoman Empire.

By contrast, the new American Zionist organization that I am contemplating here (if I may characterize it that way) will operate within the boundaries of a single already existing political jurisdiction and its members will enjoy all the rights and privileges of American citizenship: equal protection under the law, the rights of free speech and a free press, freedom of religion, freedom of association, freedom of enterprise, the right to vote, the right to bargain collectively, and, as a last resort, the right to bear arms. These differences are enormous and they are all in our favor.

iii

But even under the most favorable of circumstances there can be no doubt but that the organizational challenge before us remains formidably complex. I shall therefore now attempt to adumbrate the dimensions of that challenge as best as I can see them, which for convenience I have set out under a number of headings arranged in what I hope is some logical order.

Publicity. In the beginning was the word. People cannot possibly join this or any organization until they first hear about it. Like Herzl's *The Jewish State*, this small volume is intended to be a first step in that direction. My hope is that it will eventually attract the attention of a few dozens or perhaps hundreds of idealistic young people across the United States who are interested in founding and perhaps leading an organization of this type. The members of this vanguard will be college-educated for the most part, I would imagine, in their late twenties or early thirties, and possessed of all the talents and ambitions that will be needed in order to successfully launch a movement of this kind.

But numbers alone will not be enough. To ensure the organization's future inclusiveness, it is essential that the founding group be broadly representative of the nation as a whole, especially when it comes to region and race.[33] Not until such a representative sample has been enlisted to the cause—something that I imagine can only be accomplished by word of mouth working in conjunction with the new social media—will it be time to proceed to the founding itself.

The Founding. If the history of the World Zionist Organization is any guide, the next step will be to convene a national congress at some convenient spot in the middle of the country—Cincinnati, Ohio, would be the ideal choice in my personal opinion—where the charter and bylaws of the new corporation will be hammered out. This will be a critical moment in its history, since decisions taken at that time are bound to have repercussions in the years to come.

THE CORPORATE IMPERATIVE

As for how the corporation should be governed, here again I take a page from the history of the World Zionist Organization. I think its governance should be parliamentary in form, it being probably the most logical way to ensure that all major factions and points of view will be represented in future policy-making circles. At the same time, it is essential that diversity of opinion not be allowed to cripple the future effectiveness of the central executive. How best to reconcile these opposites is a problem for the founders to solve. My only suggestion is that they might consult Madison's *Notes of Debates in the Federal Convention of 1787*. I also hope they will at least consider adopting some of the more representative voting procedures that have been made possible by advances in computer technology.

State and Local Chapters. In a country as big and diverse as the United States, the new organization will almost certainly have to be federal in form. Much as the AFL-CIO is structured today, I foresee a federation of state and local chapters whose jurisdictions will eventually cover every state in the Union—in which case provision will have to be made in the charter and bylaws for the future inclusion of these subsidiary bodies.

Advertising. Once these organizational matters are out of the way, the next step will be to undertake a national advertising campaign employing all the resources of modern mass media. The goal will be to make the entire country aware of the organization's existence and the program it stands for. This will require a good deal of money, the raising of which will depend upon friends.

Friends and Allies. There are going to be people all over the United States who, while they may have no interest in joining themselves, will nonetheless look upon the organization with favor. Some of these individuals will be wealthy; others will occupy influential positions in society. It is imperative to reach out to these people and seek their support, and never more so than in the beginning when our financial resources are bound to be small. But at the same time, let us beware of sugar daddies. It would be a tragedy if the organization and its leadership were to be co-opted by one or a small number of donors who might not have its long-term interests at heart.

Recruitment. Recall that our new towns are to be developed gradually over a period of years, one neighborhood and one factory at a time. At the heart of this process will be the recruitment and matching of future employers with groups of qualified future homesteaders. This is a goal that can best be accomplished at the level of the metropolitan area, in my opinion. Thus, I foresee local chapters headquartered in all our major metropolitan areas and in many rural areas as well—abandoned shopping malls and big-box stores might make ideal locations—where current and prospective members will be able to come together, meet one another, socialize on a regular basis, and perhaps tentatively form themselves into future neighborhood groups. To speed this process along, it would be smart to work with existing churches, synagogues, high schools, community colleges, local unions, as well as with established civic and business organizations in the area, these being the sorts of institutions where new members and prospective employers are likely to be found.

Training and Preparation. There will almost certainly be an interval of several years between the time new members first join the organization and the day when they are fully ready and able to begin their new lives. Constructive use should be made of this interval in a number of ways:

First, as we saw at the end of the last chapter, saving money will be an essential part of the preparation process. Before a married couple can be considered for resettlement (and only married couples should be considered) they will need to have put enough money in the bank (and not just any bank but one of our own, about which I will have more to say in a moment) to purchase a lot and enough building materials to get some kind of a roof over their heads. For most couples, this will likely require several years of hard work, in which case, ironically enough, getting a part-time job in the country will turn out to be a full-time job in the city!

89

Second, the members of every future neighborhood group must be able to show that between them all they possess all the necessary skills that their future employers will require. Assuming they don't possess these skills already, they will have to acquire them one way or another: either on the job, which is generally the best way by far, or else in vocational training classes and union apprenticeship programs.

Third, every couple must be able to demonstrate basic homemaking skills: cooking, gardening, carpentry, plumbing, wiring, masonry, and the like, which they will be called on to exercise in their new lives. Those that don't possess these skills already will have to acquire them. That means enrolling in home economics and vocational training classes, whether in local high schools and community colleges or perhaps even better in the local meeting halls themselves.

Fourth, couples must be able to show that they are in stable, long-term relationships and that they know how to take care of any children they already have.

In other words, in order to fully qualify for resettlement, couples must be able to show that they possess not only the necessary grit and determination but also the right sets of skills and sufficient money to start their new lives. This is a point that cannot be overemphasized. As we saw in the last chapter, the long-term success of our towns will almost certainly depend upon the strict maintenance of a certain minimum set of standards that will apply to all participating members; and though it may sound harsh, this means without exception for reasons of race, gender, ethnicity, or other perceived disability. As with any religious organization, ours is to be a voluntary association of free individuals, and like the God of our forefathers, it will be no respecter of persons. If necessary, we must be prepared to fight for this principle in every court in the land, and we should not be deterred no matter how the courts rule.

Corporate Outreach. Offices should be established on Wall Street and advertisements and articles placed in the business press making the case for factories of the new type we propose as a way to increase the rate of return on investment in many kinds of manufacturing facilities.

Public Relations. Great care must be taken to guard our good name and to always show our true face to the public. History shows that there is rarely much progress in this world that does not involve fundamental conflicts of interest. We should therefore be ready to defend ourselves against all forms of slander, both in the courts and in the mass media. We should also be prepared to address in substance any polemical attacks launched against us by individuals and organized groups who, whether rightly or wrongly, feel that their interests are threatened. In addressing our opponents, however, let us always strive for civility while showing ourselves willing to search for compromise wherever and whenever possible.

Membership Dues. As already mentioned, this will be a dues-paying membership organization. Dues should be set high enough to cover all or most of the organization's day-to-day expenses. Whether these dues should be the same for all members or assessed on the basis of ability to pay and how they should be apportioned within the organization are matters that only the membership can decide by acting through its elected representatives.

A National Land Bank. There is one area of finance that will involve much larger sums than dues alone can possibly supply. I refer to the moneys required to purchase and develop future town sites. Here again, taking a leaf from the World Zionist Organization, I suggest we organize an institution along the lines of the Jewish National Fund, which, for those who are unfamiliar with it, raised money for the purchase of land in Palestine on which future Zionists could settle. In our case, however, instead of a charitable organization relying on voluntary contributions, I envisage something much closer to a commercial bank in which collective savings of all future homesteaders would be deposited, those deposits then being used to finance the purchase of future town sites.

When we recall that a typical garden city will require roughly one acre of land for each future inhabitant—assuming a twenty-five thousand acre town site for twenty-five thousand inhabitants—it should be clear that the loans required to purchase and develop future town sites should be well within the financial capacity of the new bank to lend. What is more, in the extremely unlikely event of a default on one of these loans due to some unforeseen but temporary circumstance, at least the town's residents could rest secure in the knowledge that the town's property would not fall into the hands of outside commercial interests who might not—indeed, almost certainly would not—have the town's long-term interests at heart.

News and Information. The membership of the new organization should have the ability not only to communicate freely among themselves but also to stay accurately informed about all important developments within the organization itself. The first of these two objectives can be easily met by means of the new social media. The second, however, is more problematic. Official websites and in-house publications will certainly be part of the mix. But even so, it is vital that truly independent sources of news and information also exist. What will be needed, in other words, are publications that are not under the direct control of the central executive, and which can therefore be relied upon to report without fear or favor all sides of any controversial issues that divide the organization and its leadership.

THE SEVENTH MILLENNIUM

Now I cannot pretend to know how such publications can be brought into existence. Maybe we should look to the origins of the *Christian Science Monitor* or of the old *Wall Street Journal* back in the days when its guiding motto was still "knowledge from facts." Even more difficult is the problem of editorial succession. The *New York Times* and the British scientific journal *Nature* furnish two cautionary tales in how not to proceed. Conceivably, this is a problem without a solution, in which case every generation will have to solve it anew.

But at least let us get it right at the start. Though it may take time, we should aim to create one or more publications that combine financial independence with the highest standards of editorial integrity, and whose goal will be to find and publish the best writers in America: the best reporters, the best investigative journalists, and the best essayists that our country can produce.

Adult Education. To promote a better understanding and a deeper appreciation of the historical roots of our movement, a program of adult education is highly desirable. This should probably take the form of a course or a series of courses in the comparative history of world civilizations, the unifying theme of which would be the long human struggle from servitude to freedom, including the gradual emergence of liberal institutions. Unfortunately, qualified teachers who can teach such courses are in very short supply nowadays, America's leading colleges and universities having largely abrogated

94

their responsibility in this area for reasons that we need not go into here.

So if there happen to be any billionaires out there who are sympathetic to our cause and would like to be remembered, they should know that there can be no better legacy, no better way of spending their money, than by endowing new colleges and universities that are dedicated to this one special task. Such liberal arts institutions are especially needed across the South and Midwest. For if enough benefactors do step forward, then the day may yet come when these two regions of the country will be able to give New England a run for its money, the spirit of Emerson having long sense died in the place of his birth.

Town Planning. Good urban planning will be essential to the success of our towns, which means that we are going to need a plentiful supply of good urban planners. Fortunately, ours is a program that by its very nature will appeal to existing schools of architecture and urban design wherever they are. It would be foolish not to reach out and cultivate these institutions. We should look to them not only for advice and ideas in the present, but as future sources of well-trained professionals. Hopefully, these schools will see in us the possibility of attracting more and better students in the years ahead, and will therefore welcome our advances.

Judicial and Legal Staff. Corporations are by law self-governing institutions. We should therefore give thought to establishing an independent judiciary within the national organization whose writ will be to protect the rights and interests of all its members; to insure the impartial enforcement of its charter and bylaws; and to oversee the good-faith execution of all policy decisions, resolutions, and initiatives that have been lawfully enacted. At the same time, looking outward, we must be prepared to defend our legal and constitutional rights wherever and whenever they are threatened. We should consider developing the requisite legal staff to meet both of these objectives.

Lobbying. As we go forward, we are going to need the services of skillful lobbyists in numbers that are sufficient to effectively represent our interests at the county, state, and federal levels of government. Issues of zoning, incorporation, eminent domain, and a wide variety of environmental, educational, and health regulations will be the focus of their efforts. The recruitment and training of such lobbyists must be anticipated.

Building a Broad Base of Popular Support. I leave for last what, in my opinion, could turn out to be the most important task of all: that of building a broad base of popular political support for our organization and the program it stands for.

THE CORPORATE IMPERATIVE

To see why this might be the case, let me tell my readers the story of another homesteading venture remarkably like the one being proposed here, right down to the notion of factories in the countryside run on part-time jobs and the idea of families building their own houses. What I want to emphasize, however, are not these striking similarities but rather what became of that earlier venture once it got started.

The story begins as a bee in the bonnet of Franklin Delano Roosevelt that had been put there by a young agricultural economist named Milburn Wilson at the start of his first administration.[34] Because the nation was then mired in the depths of the Great Depression, Milburn sold the idea to Roosevelt, who then turned around and sold it to Congress, as a way to bring much needed economic relief to hundreds of thousands of farm families scattered across the United States who suddenly found themselves stranded in the countryside with no visible means of support.

The basic idea, as Roosevelt explained it to Congress, was to create a new "rural-industrial group" that would exist as a "third type" between the "urban-industrial" and "rural-agricultural" groups of the past. To bring these rural-industrial groups into existence, he proposed that a Division of Subsistence Homesteads be set up within the newly established Resettlement Administration as part of a vast new federal program of regional planning and development. Caught up in the spirit of the times, and because it happened to be one of

97

the newly elected president's pet ideas, Congress quickly appropriated sufficient fund to launch several hundred pilot projects across the United States.

What happened next is a lesson in how not to proceed. For starters, the people selected to participate in the program were not idealistic young couples committed to the idea of pioneering a fundamentally new way of life in America. Rather, they were hardscrabble farm families who were long set in their ways and wedded to the idea their own independence. In fact, the only reason families agreed to participate in the program is that they had been promised a living wage to build their own houses, an offer that seemed almost too good to be true.

Nevertheless, trouble began right away when the participating families were informed that they would have no say in what their future homes would look like nor the manner of their construction. Instead, they would be working under the direct supervision of government officials being sent down from Washington who had been authorized to dictate not only where and how each house would be built but exactly how many rooms it would have and what the floor plan would be. In fact, it turned out there was only one floor plan! All of the houses would be identical, in other words, no consideration being given to the number of people in each family nor what their special needs might happen to be. Everything had been decided beforehand based on a plan that had been drawn up in Washington, which was fully in keeping with the paternalistic worldview and the human-engineering mindset that were so fashionable in progressive circles during that period.

Not surprisingly, this high-handed approach did not sit well with these yeoman farm families, a proud if ignorant and sometimes ornery folk who, unlike their medieval ancestors, were not used to being treated like serfs. Nor were they slow to express their displeasure, news of which soon filtered back to Washington. It was at this point that Roosevelt's pet project came under intense fire in the halls of Congress, the opposition being led by a number of well-organized business groups who were adamantly opposed to all forms of government planning as a matter of principle.

Meanwhile, as the Great Depression showed no signs of ending, Roosevelt was soon preoccupied with far bigger and more pressing concerns than the creation of rural-industrial groups. And because he and the young Milburn were the only two men in Washington who had caught the vision, as it were, the entire program was soon left without a single effective spokesman on Capitol Hill.

It is at this point that we are treated to the spectacle of a federal program without a constituency. Or rather, we are treated to the spectacle of a program whose sole constituency consisted of a few thousand poorly educated farm families scattered across the United States who were completely unorganized, leaderless, and without allies in Congress. Under these circumstances, it is hardly surprising that the program's funding was quickly and unceremoniously discontinued, leaving behind a few barely sprouted projects to wither on the ground.

I find myself thinking about those farm families whenever I drive through the hamlet of Homestead, Tennessee, which is on the Cumberland Plateau not far from where I live. Off to the side of the road in a large open field is a small group of cottages made of the local crab orchard stone. Beautifully crafted on what appear to be solid foundations, they stand as a mute memorial to Roosevelt's all-but-forgotten dream.

One of the lessons I draw from this story is that in in a democracy like ours, it pays to have a broad base of popular political support. It is not enough "that your cause it is just" in the words of the old Bob Dylan song. It doesn't even matter that the President of the United States is on your side. If powerful interests are organized against you, then unless your side is organized as well—and you have the numbers to boot!—there is little chance that your side will prevail.

With that lesson in mind, how might we go about building such a broad base of popular political support? The only answer I can think of is that we are going to have to make ourselves into the champion of the interests of all working-class people in America regardless of whether they are interested in the new way of life for themselves (or for their children and grandchildren) *and we must be seen as such in the eyes of the public.* To that end and without going into detail, here are seven planks in a platform that we might place before the public:

THE CORPORATE IMPERATIVE

First, a *wage-price equalization tax* or tariff on all imported goods and services that are produced in countries with wage-rates much lower than ours, such a tax being the only way to level the playing field on which American workers are expected to compete. In defense of such a tax, we shall argue that the theory of free trade never included free mobility of capital across international boundaries; that Adam Smith specifically opposed direct foreign investment as detrimental to the wealth of a nation; that David Ricardo never imagined a world of high- and low-wage countries in which wage arbitrage would be the major motive for trade; and last but not least, that all the other "comparative advantages" of trade that Ricardo identified or that are commonly associated with his name would continue to exist, including those arising from differences of climate, access to natural resources, industrial specialization, and the particular strengths and weaknesses of the workers in any given country.

Second, an across-the-board moratorium (pause, time-out) on further immigration into the United States until we can show we know how to assimilate and integrate the seventy-five million or so first- and second-generation immigrants who are already here (including eleven to twenty million undocumented), the vast majority from societies and cultures with no, or very weak, democratic traditions. In the meantime, in the interest of maximum global welfare, we should look into the question of whether immigration to the United States helps or hurts the development of the poor countries from which most immigrants come. Instead of draining these countries of their scarce human capital, mightn't it be better to redirect the stream of emigration, above all of high-skilled emigration, in the opposite direction?

Third, a biometric Social Security card for all American citizens and legal immigrants as the only realistic way to enforce our nation's immigration laws. This card would serve as proof of legal status to be in this country and would have to be presented in order to hold a job, open a bank account, cash or write a check, use a credit card, get a driver's license, vote, sign a contract, or otherwise carry on the normal activities of everyday life. Foreign visitors without the right to work in this country could be issued biometric visas clarifying their legal status.

Fourth, a family-friendly six-hour day and thirty-hour work week (including triple pay for overtime to show we mean business). As Samuel Gompers argued a hundred years ago, the answer to the introduction of a never-ending stream of new labor-saving technologies is a consonant reduction in the hours of labor, that being not only the fairest but also the most natural way to adjust to the decline in the demand for labor and thus share in the gains brought about by technological progress.[35] The eight-hour day and forty-hour week that were enacted into

102

law eighty years ago as part of the Fair Labor Standards Act are by now long out of date.

Fifth, treaties with our major allies and trading partners (all OECD countries) outlawing shell corporations and unregistered bank and brokerage accounts in overseas tax havens. These two reforms can be justified as being necessary in order for a country to collect the taxes it is legally owed, which is a need that all countries share. They are further justified as a way to deny criminal organizations (both foreign and domestic) access to the international financial system. The transition to a largely cashless society, which is already well underway, should also be further encouraged for the same reasons. Furthermore, when taken together, these three reforms would open the way to the sixth plank in our platform.

Sixth, a graduated expenditure tax (which is like a graduated income tax but with savings tax-exempt) to replace all other forms of taxation, including taxes on capital gains, interest, estates, corporations, real estate, and sales. The basic idea is to progressively tax the spending of the biggest consumers in society while ignoring inequalities of income and wealth. We shall argue that a graduated expenditure tax is the only fair and efficient way to finance a whole-scale redistribution of income from capital (including human capital) to labor that does not simultaneously reduce the incentives to work, save, and invest, especially among the entrepreneurial class, as it actually increases them instead.

Seventh, an improved and expanded version of the earned income tax credit big enough to compensate the less-skilled workers in our society not only for the losses they have incurred as a result of changes Congress made in America's trade and immigration laws over the past fifty years, but also for those caused by a never-ending stream of new labor-saving technologies. If we are going to maintain an open, technologically innovative global economy (and let us pray that we do), it is time for economists to acknowledge that *the principle of compensation* has always been an integral part of the theory of free trade[36] and, what is more, that the same logic applies when it comes to addressing inequalities brought about by mass low-skilled immigration and advancing technology.

Playing the Game. In today's media-driven campaigns for high public office, the great game of politics is one that most of our citizens have forgotten how to play. The art of contesting an election can be tremendous fun—indeed, one of the supreme forms of entertainment—and never more so than when your side is winning.

My parents, who were active in the American labor movement in the 1940s and '50s, played that game with gusto in the mid-sized industrial city of Chattanooga where I grew up. I can still remember as a child the gay parties that took place at our house whenever election season rolled around. It was then that the long metal file boxes would come out from wherever they had been hiding, and a small army of volunteers would gather around our dining room table to receive their instructions. Their goal was to canvass door to door every house in every neighborhood in every precinct in the city. Organized labor was a force to be reckoned with back then. It can become so again.

But if our immediate goal will be to win the next election, the ultimate goal is something much grander: to bring about what Cicero once referred to as a "concordance of classes," which in today's world would mean establishing a balance of power between land and labor on the one side and capital on the other[37] in the long-term interests of our whole civilization.

iv

I would like to conclude this forth and final chapter with a few words of caution addressed to all future members of the new corporation who, like the author, long for the day. Only we can take ourselves to the promised land. Nobody else can do it for us. Only if we march together in good order and good cheer—and have fun along the way—will we arrive at a place of which it can be said:

105

THE SEVENTH MILLENNIUM

*Here is the true economy; the ground of culture;
the field of enlightenment.*

And as we travel together towards that near-distant
goal let us teach our children the original, pure religion of
Abraham[38] and to never forget the generations of their
ancestors before them, drawn from the four quarters of the
globe. For it was their sacrifice alone—both willing and
unwilling—that makes everything possible. We must
always remember them lest we slip back into the hellhole
of history from which they delivered us.

Appendices

I.

The Gallup Report

July 16, 1976

Arthur L. Keiser
Executive Vice President
The Gallup Organization, Inc.
Marketing and Attitude Research
53 Bank Street
Princeton, New Jersey

Mr. Luke Lea, President
The Southern Rural Development Corporation
1108 North Concord Road
Chattanooga, Tennessee 34741

Dear Mr. Lea:

We are enclosing additional tabulations for your study.
There will be no extra charge for them.

You will see that we show ten-year spans by age groups
rather than 65 years and older as requested. From the
figures you can, of course, see how the various older
groups respond. Also shown are results by education—
those who have attended college, those with a high school
education and those with less than high school. The
tabulations by income group may also be of interest.

With best wishes,

Arthur L. Keiser

THE SEVENTH MILLENNIUM

The question:

As a new way to live in America, the idea has been suggested of building factories in rural areas—away from cities—and running them on part-time jobs. Under this arrangement the man and the woman would each work 3 days a week 6 hours a day. People would have enough spare time to build their own houses, to cultivate a garden and for hobbies and other outside interests.

How interested would you be in this way of life: definitely interested, probably interested, probably not interested, definitely not interested?

	Breakdown of those over 50 years of age		
	50-59 yrs.	60-69 yrs.	70 yrs. and older
	%	%	%
Definitely interested	16	12	13
Probably interested	22	22	20
Probably not interested	18	18	11
Definitely not interested	38	38	44
Don't Know	6	10	12
	100	100	100
Number of Interviews	252	208	149

110

THE GALLUP REPORT

	College	High School	Grade School
	%	%	%
Definitely interested	15	16	18
Probably interested	27	23	21
Probably not interested	22	20	10
Definitely not interested	32	36	40
Don't Know	4	5	11
	100	100	100
Number of Interviews	511	783	227

THE SEVENTH MILLENNIUM

<u>By Annual Family Income</u>

	$20,000 or more	$12,000– $19,999	$10,000– $11,999	Under $10,000
	%	%	%	%
Definitely interested	9	13	18	22
Probably interested	22	25	26	22
Probably not interested	27	19	21	15
Definitely not interested	40	38	32	32
Don't Know	2	5	3	9
	100	100	100	100
Number of Interviews	339	465	138	531

The Public's Attitudes Towards a New Way to Live in America

The sample of adults interviewed represents about 145,000,000 people (the civilian-non-institutional population, eighteen years of age and older). The question asked:

> As a new way to live in America, the idea has been suggested of building factories in rural areas—away from cities—and running them on part-time jobs. Under this arrangement the man and the woman would each work 3 days a week 6 hours a day. People would have enough spare time to build their own houses, to cultivate a garden and for hobbies and other outside interests.

> How interested would you be in this way of life: definitely interested, probably interested, probably not interested, definitely not interested?

THE FINDINGS

A total of about four of every ten people interviewed expressed some interest in this new way of life. About one of every six people (16%) interviewed answered "Definitely interested" and about one of every four people

(28%) said "Probably interested." Since the sample of adults interviewed represents about 145,000,000 people (the civilian-non-institutional population, eighteen years of age and older), it can be said that 58,000,000 people expressed some interest (either "definitely" or "probably interested"). The exact division of replies was as follows:

	Per Cent
Definitely interested	16
Probably interested	24
Probably not interested	19
Definitely not interested	35
Don't Know	6
	100
Number of Interviews	1524

THE GALLUP REPORT

The tabulations by sex show that somewhat more of the men than of the women are "Definitely not interested." Replies divided by sex as follows:

	Men	Women
	%	%
Definitely interested	17	16
Probably interested	21	26
Probably not interested	19	19
Definitely not interested	38	33
Don't Know	5	6
	100	100
Number of Interviews	763	761

THE SEVENTH MILLENNIUM

When the results were examined by age groups, it was found that there was more interest among young adults than older people. Replies by age groups follow:

	18–24 yrs. %	25–34 yrs. %	35–49 yrs. %	50 yrs. & older %
Definitely interested	18	19	15	14
Probably interested	29	25	23	21
Probably not interested	19	19	24	16
Definitely not interested	32	32	34	40
Don't Know	2	5	4	9
	100	100	100	100
Number of Interviews	224	336	345	609

116

THE GALLUP REPORT

Non-whites were considerably more interested in the plan than the white people interviewed.

	White %	Non-White %
Definitely interested	14	34
Probably interested	24	27
Probably not interested	20	11
Definitely not interested	37	20
Don't Know	5	8
	100	100
Number of Interviews	1370	154

THE SEVENTH MILLENNIUM

Analyses of the results by size of community show that people in the cities are somewhat more interested in the idea than those in the smaller towns and rural areas.

	1,000,000 or more %	250,000– 999,999 %	50,000– 249,999 %	2,500– 49,000 %	Under 2,500 %
Definitely interested	16	25	16	13	12
Probably interested	24	24	24	21	25
Probably not interested	19	17	19	22	19
Definitely not interested	32	32	38	40	36
Don't Know	9	2	3	4	8
	100	100	100	100	100
Number of Interviews	297	299	284	251	393

THE GALLUP REPORT

As reported below, the proportion of those who are "Definitely Interested" is greater in the South than in other regions of the country.

	East %	Mid-West %	South %	West %
Definitely interested	14	13	20	18
Probably interested	30	22	19	25
Probably not interested	17	18	22	18
Definitely not interested	34	41	32	34
Don't Know	5	6	7	5
	100	100	100	100
Number of Interviews	442	438	409	235

119

II.
But Why Factories?

Probably the most frequently asked question I've gotten over the years is, Why factories? Are factories really necessary for an idea like this to work? The answer is yes, factories really are necessary—and the reason is that with a few notable exceptions it is impossible to have a politically independent town in the countryside that does not export goods and services *at least* equal in value to those that it imports and consumes. To see why this is so, it helps to look at the exceptions:

State capitals, like Frankfort, Kentucky, which rely on revenues generated by taxing the incomes of people who live and work in other parts of the state.

College towns, like Princeton, New Jersey, which rely on student tuitions and income from endowments.

Tourist towns, like Gatlinburg, Tennessee, which rely on the spending of visitors who live and work elsewhere.

Resort towns, like Aspen, Colorado, which rely on the spending of wealthy elites whose incomes are generated elsewhere.

Commuter towns, like Signal Mountain, Tennessee, which rely on money earned by residents who work in a nearby city, in this case Chattanooga.

Retirement communities, like those found in Florida, which rely on spending financed by Social Security, private pensions, and life savings.

Future but as yet non-existant communities that rely on earned income tax credits financed by taxing the incomes of the better-off members of society, most of whom live and work elsewhere.[39]

III.
Some Unresolved Issues

There are a number of issues that I have not addressed in these pages, not because they aren't important or I haven't thought about them, but because I either see no single or best answer or am unsure of what the right answer is.

For example: How will family homesteads be handed down from one generation to the next? Which child will inherit—the youngest, the oldest, the son, or the daughter? And which will have to find a new place to live? What if a couple leaves no children behind? Will families be free to sell their homesteads in one neighborhood and trade up or down for another in a different part of town? What about a family that wants to quit the town altogether? Will it be free to sell its property to the highest bidder, even to an out-of-town stranger, or will the sale be subject to town and/or neighborhood approval as we see in the case of Manhattan co-op apartments? What about a town or neighborhood resident who commits first-degree murder or some other major criminal offense? Will he (or she) be allowed to resume residence in the town or neighborhood once his sentence has been served, or will he be subject to shunning and/or exile? I have no doubt that different communities are going to answer these and many other similarly difficult questions in a variety of ways. Local politics are bound to be interesting.

Medical care is another subject I have not touched upon (apart from end-of-life care) even though it is apparent that our current health-care system is eating us alive. Assuming private health insurance plans continue to exist, will community risk pools be organized at the town level? How about walk-in infirmaries dispensing routine care at prices far below what is customary in our big cities today? What about Workers' Compensation and Social Security disability insurance, both of which are rife with fraud in a society as large and diverse as ours, and the premiums for which are a direct cost of labor. Will there be community rating and local self-policing of fraudulent claims? And if so, how big of an increase in hourly take-home pay are workers likely to realize as a result?

Another important question is whether each town shall have exclusive rights to work in the factories in its jurisdiction. This is a complicated issue, and while I may be mistaken I would argue that it must have this right. For otherwise, there will be nothing to prevent employers bringing in outside workers as a way to drive down wages and possibly destroy the town's viability as an independent community. A closely related question is, How free should long-established manufacturers in a community be to simply pick up and leave lock, stock, and barrel, no questions asked? Again, I am not sure what the best answer is.

SOME UNRESOLVED ISSUES

A related issue is whether a town's residents should be free to move from one employer to another within the town's jurisdiction. I would argue that they must have this right and that employers (or at least manufacturers) should be obliged to hire them in accordance with the formula I described in my Note on Wages and Prices. Otherwise, involuntary unemployment and significant wage inequalities are bound to arise over time as a consequence of the changing fortunes of various industries and companies in an ever-changing world.

Another set of issues concerns the cultural and demographic relationship between the new towns and the various big cities around which they will cluster. One question in particular is whether community standards of decency should be made uniform throughout the nation as a matter of constitutional law (as the Supreme Court of late has been inclined to rule) or whether these standards should be allowed to vary in the interests of greater tolerance and diversity. Not entirely unrelated is the question of whether America's big cities are going to continue to function as population sinks the way they do now. If the answer is yes, should the new towns take it upon themselves to make up the difference by encouraging out-migration in limited amounts and above replacement levels of fertility? And if the answer is no, then how will the upper-middle class that lives in every big city—and who are a vital element in the functioning of any complex industrial society—be replenished?

Demography being destiny, this will be an issue that cannot be ignored.

And then there is the larger civilizational issue I raised in the preface, particularly as it relates America's role in the world. The central idea of this book around which everything revolves—I mean of course the idea of factories in the countryside run on part-time jobs—is of such a general nature that there is no reason to think it might not work as an engine of reform not only in other advanced Western-style democracies but in many of the less-developed parts of the world as well: in the middle-income countries of Eastern Europe and Latin America most obviously, but also eventually throughout Asia as well. Indeed, it is not inconceivable that factories of the new type being proposed could be made to operate profitably in the tribal areas of Africa and the Middle East, where they might provide an alternative path to development. This raises an interesting question: How involved should we get in supporting similar movements in other parts of the world? Of course we should offer our moral support. That goes without saying. But beyond that, and with the single exception of Mexico (and perhaps the several small countries of Central America), I am inclined to advise that we focus our energies on successfully realizing the dream here at home, believing as I do that the source of America's influence in the world has always lain in the example it can set in the field of human possibility.

IV.
GATT JUSTICE: Who Gets the Gains
of Trade?

[The following article was originally commissioned by *Harper's* magazine in late 1993 and after being rejected as "insufficiently journalistic" and "unsuitable for a general audience"—its editor, Lewis Lapham, asked the writer to "dumb it down" (his words) and make it more relevant to the more immediate future, which he refused to do— was eventually published in *Challenge* magazine, Volume 37, a year later.]

Without a fair and efficient way to bring about a wholesale redistribution of income from capital to labor, most Americans would be better off to reject free trade out of hand.

> *"I would never knowingly do anything to hurt the job market in America . . . I ran for this job to alleviate the insecurity, the anxiety, the anger, the frustrations of ordinary Americans."*

> —President Clinton, November 9, 1993, on the eve of the famous NAFTA debate between Ross Perot and Vice President Gore

In the aftermath of the Cold War, with communism having been relegated to the dust bin of history and the capitalist ideal triumphant everywhere, we awaken to find the West moving rapidly to embrace the idea of free trade in the new global economy. Last year's NAFTA and this year's GATT are but two milestones along the way. They lend substance to the idea that not only will market economies soon blanket the earth, but a new golden age of laissez-faire is at hand, one whose watchwords will be free markets, free trade, and free mobility of capital around the world. "The tectonic forces of integration" waxed one bard on Wall Street, "have shifted irrevocably."

There are a number of reasons why this is happening. Opportunities to make money overseas are obviously not to be discounted any more than are the natural urges of statesmen to act on a grand scale. But one big reason is that economists have persuaded Western political leaders that free trade will lead to gains in the efficiency with which every country's economic resources are used—gains that, in theory at least, can make all citizens in every country better off than before and that will greatly speed the development of the poorer parts of the globe. It sounds good, or even better than good, yet the ordinary citizen has no way of judging. Permit me, therefore, a simple gardener with no axe to grind—a voice of unorganized labor, if you will—to take the reader on a cook's tour of contemporary trade theory in language that the layman can understand. My purpose will be to see whether such claims are justified and, if so, under what circumstances and subject to what conditions. The results, I dare say, will surprise you.

GATT JUSTICE: WHO GETS THE GAINS OF TRADE?

Definition of terms

But first, following Voltaire, let us define our terms. By *free trade* I mean the notion that nations are better off, on balance, not to tax or otherwise impede the flows of goods and services across their borders, with exceptions always being made for things such as gun running, shipments of cocaine, child pornography, or the decampment of boatloads of illegal immigrants off the Jersey shore.

This is, of course, one of the oldest and most widely accepted axioms in economics. Adam Smith, for example, was already propounding the doctrine as early as 1776 in that *annus mirabilis* of the Scottish enlightenment, when *The Wealth of Nations* appeared alongside the Declaration of Independence. Smith's argument was in essence quite simple. It boiled down to saying that voluntary exchange between individuals must, as a rule, be mutually beneficial, or else the exchange would never take place. The mere fact that two individuals happened to reside in different countries could have no bearing on the matter. This had the ring of the self-evident and, doubtless, did much to shatter the mercantile prejudices of his age.

Forty years were to pass, however, before another amateur British economist of genius, this one a retired stock-exchange speculator named David Ricardo, put trade theory on the map for good. He did it by extending Smith's original insight to cover the case of countries that aren't content merely to exchange the goods they already possess, but that deliberately set out to produce them for one another's markets. Ricardo's starting point was also rather simple. He noted that countries differ in the "relative efficiencies" with which they make various things. He measured efficiency here by the value of the inputs (in this case man-hours, since he subscribed to the labor theory of value) that it takes to produce a dollar's worth of output. Just as individuals differ in their talents, meaning that some people are able to do some things better than others, so it is with countries. Ricardo ascribed these differences between nations to variations in climate, natural resources, and to the knowledge and skills that different groups of people bring to their tasks. The French, for example, have both the climate and the know-how to make wine. He then went on to prove by algebra that countries will be better off (will enjoy more of everything at lower prices) if they specialize in those things they do better than others. He showed this to be true even if one country (owing to the superior talents of its people, let us say) was absolutely more efficient in every line of production than all the others. This insight, so counterintuitive on its face—that we can be better off by paying others to do things we know how to do better ourselves—is called the principle of comparative advantage, and it won for Ricardo everlasting fame. Indeed, it is no understatement to say that from Ricardo's day forward, enlightened opinion everywhere has subscribed to the idea of free trade, and that his principle of comparative advantage has been the chief weapon used to combat the claims of special interests everywhere who plead for high tariffs to protect their relatively less-efficient enterprises against foreign competition.

Winners and losers

Yet as both Smith and Ricardo knew full well those special interests were the flies in the ointment of the theory of free trade. Because of them one could not argue that free trade would *automatically* make everyone better off than before, at least not in the short run. Some groups could suffer immediate and perhaps irremediable harm. Workers employed in those enterprises that are no longer competitive, for example, would be thrown out of work; businessmen whose capital is employed in such enterprises could see the value of their investments shrivel to zero. Factories and skills that, on Monday, were serviceable enough, were providing livelihoods to ordinary hands, and were earning a decent rate of profit for their owners could turn out, on Friday, to be quite obsolete.

In short free trade produced both winners and losers. On the positive side there was no question that it would benefit those people who consume the articles that henceforth could be purchased more cheaply from abroad. They would experience the unalloyed pleasure that comes from a decline in their cost of living (call it the Walmart effect). However, on the negative side, honesty required one to admit that free trade could also devastate the lives and fortunes of those people who formerly produced those articles in the home economy. And of course it often turns out, at least in our own day and age (though, interestingly enough, not in Ricardo's), that the people who consume and the people who produce are one and the same.

The way the classical economists chose to deal with this problem was, as we might expect, eminently sensible. They urged caution. They especially urged caution in the case of countries whose manufacturing industries had, for whatever reason, grown up behind high barriers to trade—whether because of a history of high tariffs, long-standing political hostilities abroad, or the mere absence of reliable transportation and communications facilities linking overseas markets. In such circumstances, they counseled, the barriers to trade should come down slowly and by degrees, so as to give the people whose livelihoods might be adversely affected a chance to adjust. For workers, this meant gradually leaving their old places of employment in declining industries and finding new work and learning new skills in those industries that, because of their comparative advantage in the new international marketplace, would be expanding. It was the same for businessmen. Adjustment meant giving them time to depreciate their plant and equipment (by wearing it out). They would be allowed to redirect their capital into new lines of activity instead of refurbishing existing factories. In this way (or so reasoned Smith, Ricardo, and, later, John Stuart Mill, the last of the great trio of classical

GATT JUSTICE: WHO GETS THE GAINS OF TRADE?

British economists), it should be possible to minimize the harm done to the losers under free trade, and eventually to reach a point where everyone could benefit. Indeed, Adam Smith, in *The Wealth of Nations*, held, "It may be desirable to introduce freedom of trade by slow gradations." Thus would the general welfare of society be unmistakably improved.

I think most economists would accept this as a fair and accurate description of the classical doctrine of free trade. Moreover, I doubt many will accuse me of bias when I say that this is the form of the doctrine they first learned in school, and from which its immense intellectual prestige is derived. Indeed, with but minor modifications, it is in terms such as these that free trade is understood and approved by most educated opinion today. If you doubt it, look no further than to the countless editorials that were written in favor of NAFTA last fall; the ones in *The New Republic* and *Nature* were representative. Or take note of the current controversies surrounding GATT.

It may come as a surprise to most laypersons to learn, therefore, that this classical doctrine of free trade has almost nothing to do with the way modern economists think about trade. Indeed, classical free trade theory has about as much resemblance to modern trade theory as classical physics has to the modern theory of quantum mechanics.

133

The role of capital

If we were to point out the single thing that distinguishes modern trade theory from that of the classical economists, it would have to be capital—the role capital plays in production, how vast disparities in capital between nations can generate trade between them, and the effect such trade will have upon the distribution of income in those nations.

The classical economists (as I've already noted in the case of Ricardo) subscribed to the labor theory of value. For them, this meant that labor was the only recognized factor of production. Some goods cost more than others because different amounts of labor were required to produce them. The idea that capital—which is to say, tools together with a people's knowledge of how to use and make them—was also an important ingredient in production was alien to them. In fact, the very word *capital* as used by the classical economists usually referred to *corn*—meaning the surpluses of grain and other food stocks that had been accumulated from the previous year's harvest and that were thenceforth available to feed work crews to build roads, drain swamps, and undertake other such "capital" improvements. Of course, the classical economists were aware that there were novel forms of capital on the scene. The new steam engines, railroads, and textile machinery could hardly have escaped their notice. Yet they had no way of incorporating these novelties into their theory of

134

exchange; they had no way of knowing (Ecclesiastes to
the contrary notwithstanding) that vast accumulations of
capital in the form of modern technology represented
something fundamentally new under the sun.

The classical economists were also hobbled by
another idea. They subscribed to Thomas Malthus's idea
of the iron law of wages. This was the notion that the pay
received by ordinary working people could never rise
above the bare minimum needed to sustain life.
According to Malthus, if wages rose above the
subsistence level, the workers would breed until their
numbers bid the price of labor back down. For this reason,
it was impossible for them to conceive of a world in
which the workers in one country would be paid many
times more than the workers in another. The whole world
was underdeveloped in those days, and the notion that
some nations might grow rich (in the sense of their
"laboring classes" being able to enjoy modest degrees of
leisure and affluence) was simply more than their
imaginations could comprehend. Incidentally, this is why
the free trade debate in the last century was relatively
little concerned with the welfare of ordinary working
people; it was mostly about how free trade would benefit
the small number of elites at the top of society—the
landed aristocracy on the one hand and the emerging
bourgeoisie on the other—who alone commanded the
discretionary incomes necessary to purchase cheap

foreign commodities. Not for nothing did economics become known as the dismal science.

A revolutionary thesis

But all this began to change in the last quarter of the nineteenth century. It was swept away by the undeniable progress of society (ordinary wages were clearly rising above the subsistence level) and by a revolution in the way economists looked at the process of production. For the first time, they began to understand the contribution that capital was making to wages. We call this revolution the *neoclassical* or *marginalist* revolution in economics, and it became, in effect, the quantum mechanics of all subsequent economic thinking.

At the heart of the neoclassical revolution was the recognition that labor, by itself, could produce little; but, when given tools and materials to work with, it could produce a great deal. Furthermore, it was realized that the more tools a population had at its disposal the more productive it would be, subject only to the law of diminishing returns. In short, tools were important, and more tools were better.

Nor was this all. When looked at from the other side, it turned out that the situation was exactly symmetrical with respect to capital. In other words, capital by itself could produce nothing. However, in the hands of labor, it could produce something. The more laborers there were for a given stock of capital, the more

136

productive the capital would be, again subject to the same law of diminishing returns.

Economists put these two ideas together and called it the *law of variable proportions*. Most importantly, they were able to show (to prove by algebra once again) that in a market economy the rewards of labor and capital were set equal to their respective marginal productivities, which in turn were determined by their relative proportions. This law applied not just to any particular industries or places of employment but throughout society as a whole. Thus, the more capital a country had for a given population, the higher the wages would be, and the lower the profits. But the more workers there were for a given quantity of capital, the higher the profits would be, and the lower the wages. When wages went up, profits went down, and vice versa. The progress of wages could thus be explained by the fact that vast accumulations of capital were taking place in society, raising the average marginal productivity of labor.

Implications for trade

None of this had much to do with trade, of course, but it did raise an interesting question. If some countries were gradually growing wealthy while others remained poor, what prevented the capitalists from taking their capital out of the wealthy areas and investing it overseas, where the law of variable proportions would work to their favor?

137

THE SEVENTH MILLENNIUM

As a matter of fact, a good deal of this did go on. But it was confined largely to Western Europe and to the United States for the simple reason that these were the only countries with all the necessary institutions required to make markets work. Above all, they had strong central governments committed to making them work. England invested in Germany and vice versa. (Some may remember that Engels owned a factory in Manchester.) Moreover, both countries invested in the United States. Gradually, the whole West European cultural area grew rich. Meanwhile, such commercial goings-on that touched the relatively "backward" areas of Asia, Africa, and Latin America were either rapacious in character (the slave trade, the East India Company, the opium wars), or else were intended to extract scarce raw materials and agricultural produce unavailable at home. These operations in foreign markets were concentrated around the peripheries, where harbors could be built. The interiors of these continents remained largely without roads, communications, or even the basic institutions needed to make individuals secure in their persons and property.

Meanwhile, the economists too were busy trying to work out the implications of the neoclassical revolution for international trade, especially as it related to trade between rich countries and poor countries (i.e., between populations that had lots of capital and populations that had little). It took them a long time. In fact, it was not until the first quarter of the twentieth century that two

138

GATT JUSTICE: WHO GETS THE GAINS OF TRADE?

Swedes named Heckscher and Ohlin got the first glimpse of an answer. And it was not until mid-century that Paul Samuelson, the enfant terrible of American mathematical economists (and the man who wrote the textbook we all used in college), drew their insights to a logical conclusion. The results were theoretically surprising and, for workers in the West, ominous in the extreme—so surprising and so ominous in fact that to this day many otherwise well trained economists are unable to believe them.

In essence, Samuelson found that it would make little difference whether capital were free to move between rich countries and poor. Trade alone could bring about much the same result. In other words, under free trade, wages could be expected to fall and profits to rise in the rich countries, just as it would happen if large amounts of capital were shifted overseas. The way it worked was that low-wage countries would specialize in labor-intensive goods (where they enjoyed a comparative advantage), leaving the rich countries to specialize in goods that required little labor and much capital. The effect would be to lower the demand for labor and raise the demand for capital in the rich countries. That would cause wages to fall and profits to rise. This effect was limited only by the gap in wages between the two sets of countries (the bigger the gap the more wages could fall) and by whether complete specialization occurred.

139

In fact, Samuelson was able to prove (using algebra once again) that as a rule wages and profits would be equalized around the world at points somewhere midway between the rates that initially prevailed in the rich and poor countries before trading began. Indeed, much the same result would accrue if capital were completely free to move among them. The only difference was that without capital mobility wages and profits would both end up slightly lower owing to the extra transportation costs incurred when trade is the only mechanism for bringing about equality. The name of this finding is the *factor-price equalization theorem*, and it seems destined to become one of the most celebrated and controversial results in the whole history of economics, certainly in this century.

But, of course, so long as there was relatively little trade in practice between the rich and poor countries (or little mobility of capital either, for that matter), the controversy was largely academic, and could be quietly confined to the economics departments of our leading universities. But all that changed in the years between 1987 and 1991. With the collapse of the Soviet Union, the West woke up one morning to discover that communism, its erstwhile ideological nemesis and a political force to be reckoned with around the globe for over three generations, had unexpectedly disappeared. Virtually overnight, it seemed, Marxism had ceased to exist as an armed and credible creed in the world. This was true not only in Russia and in the formerly captive nations of

GATT JUSTICE: WHO GETS THE GAINS OF
TRADE?

Eastern Europe but even more importantly throughout Asia, Africa, and Latin America.

For their part, the leaders of dozens of former "second-" and "third-world" countries (now known collectively as the *developing world*) could see the handwriting on the wall. They were busy getting over their hostility to the West and began to put aside any misgivings they might have formerly expressed about capitalism. Such feelings were henceforth to be dismissed as relics of the colonial and neocolonial past. Portraits of Karl Marx were being torn down from their places in the public squares, even as neckties sporting Adam Smith's picture on them were appearing around the necks of their newly suited business classes. Most important of all, policies were changing. The poor countries were unilaterally slashing their tariffs, joining GATT, and unabashedly clamoring for Western trade and investment. It soon became clear that they wished to ape the "export-led" growth strategies that had been pioneered by the little tigers of East Asia.

But these were no little tigers. Two of them—China and India—had forty percent of the world's people (twice the total population of the West) who were willing to work for less than a dollar per hour. In China's case, furthermore, it was apparent that a strong central government was now in place that was absolutely committed to making markets work. Networks of roads, power stations, and wireless communications systems were springing up like crazy. A stock market was opened up (along with a high-fashion industry) and a central banking system (albeit state owned) was established. Theft and assault were made capital offenses. In short, all the barriers that formerly had prevented large-scale trade and investment with the West—political, institutional, technical, and economic—were giving way simultaneously. It was as if the Hoover Dam had burst.

Impact on workers

Strangely, however, economists in the West were silent about the implications of this development for Western workers. They were urging none of the caution their classical forbears might have been expected to counsel in a similar situation. On the contrary, they seemed to be caught up in the same spirit of euphoria that was gripping the business, media, and political elites at the time. A perfect example of this was the highly influential letter sent to President Clinton last fall by 300 leading U.S. economists (including fourteen Nobel Prize winners) endorsing the North American Free Trade Agreement with Mexico. NAFTA, as the reader will recall, is designed to remove all trade and investment barriers with our poor and populous neighbor to the south. It was sold to Congress as a prelude to this year's GATT accords (encompassing both China and India) and to similar agreements to be negotiated in the near future with the rest of Latin America. After NAFTA would come

142

GATT JUSTICE: WHO GETS THE GAINS OF TRADE?

AFTA—a truly all-American free-trade zone stretching from the Arctic Circle to the tip of Tierra Del Fuego.

What was most curious about the economists' letter to Clinton was its pretension to being a balanced appraisal—a weighing of the costs against the benefits—where the issue was free trade between rich and poor countries. Yet it opened with a standard piece of nineteenth-century boilerplate ("an open trading relationship directly benefits all consumers"). It featured the observation that the gains to the winners would more than offset any losses to the losers. No mention was made of the fact that most consumers nowadays are workers too, and that the wages of the overwhelming majority of workers could be expected to fall even faster than prices. That is precisely what it means to say that real wages decline. In other words, the economists forgot to say that the Walmart effect would be more than offset by the McJobs effect. Nor was it pointed out to President Clinton that any gains in the nation's total output, and hence in the average incomes of American citizens, would be swamped by a wholesale redistribution of income from capital to labor. Typically, for every dollar of gain, several dollars of income would be taken away from ordinary working people (the low- and semi-skilled) and given to a privileged stratum at the top of society composed primarily of people with superior educations and significant capital holdings. It was as though Messrs. Heckscher and Ohlin had never been born.

THE SEVENTH MILLENNIUM

Even more bizarre was a statement by Paul Samuelson himself—the king of the mathematical economists—delivered last October before an august assemblage in the East Room of the White House. Henry Kissinger was there along with President Clinton and six other Nobel Laureates. They all supported NAFTA. When Prof. Samuelson stepped to the microphone, he simply said that "protection had never resulted in a net increase in the number of high-paying jobs." This coming from the same man who fifty years earlier had created a sensation in the economics profession by proving (in the celebrated Stolper–Samuelson theorem) that a tariff on labor-intensive goods imported from poor countries could prop up the wages of workers in a high-wage economy. That the good professor was being disingenuous, therefore, was the kindest thing one could say; it was enough to give his profession a bad name.

Clearly, something was going on here that cries out for explanation. Why would the world's leading economists choose to mislead the leader of a great democracy on an issue of such overriding importance to the majority of its citizens? Did they wish to bankrupt the welfare state and torpedo the liberal consensus that, since the days of Franklin Delano Roosevelt, had bound up the rift between labor and capital? Was it of no consequence to them that the bottom four-fifths of American families (who were already stretched in their ability to care for their children and old people, and whose wages had already been declining for more than two decades) should see their whole way of life unravel? How could national health insurance ever become a reality if, like Medicare, it were financed out of wages at a time when the wage-base was collapsing? Or were the people of the United States, having climbed from underdevelopment to a middle-class standard of living, to be consigned once more to the abyss?

Very few economists, I think, would answer this last question in the affirmative. Not even Milton Friedman at his most libertarian subscribes to what a recent letter-writer to the *Wall Street Journal* was pleased to call "the justice of the market place." Indeed, few flinty Presbyterians remain, even in the windy city of Chicago, who can take comfort in the words of St. Matthew, that "to them that hath shall be given, and from them that hath not shall be taken away, even the little that they hath."

A "value-free" objectivity

Was the problem that, nowadays, too many economists adopt the pretense of being scientists? Were they, in the name of objectivity—or what the Germans call being *wertfrei* (value free)—enjoying the luxury of not having to make difficult judgments involving "interpersonal comparisons" between individuals? Certainly, many economists think this way. At least they used to earlier in the century. For them the possibility that a skewing of the distribution of income might adversely affect the general welfare of society could be sidestepped, along with such quaint notions as a dollar being worth more to a poor man than a rich one. They could take cover behind a convenient agnosticism and be content to point out that, whenever total income goes up, at least the physical potential exists to make everyone better off than before. For them this became their minimum, indeed their only criterion in such matters.

Pareto optimality is the technical term for this criterion. Economists use Pareto optimality to justify changes in the economy that can, in principle at least, make some people better off without making anyone else worse off. Changes that meet this criterion are said to increase the efficiency of the economy. The trouble is that Pareto optimality can theoretically be used to justify maintaining a state of affairs in which the entire wealth of a society is in the hands of a single individual, leaving the rest of society with no wealth at all. Thus, what was originally conceived to be a noncontroversial (in the sense of value free) criterion for advocating change turns out to be extraordinarily controversial.

But I doubt that this ideal of their science being value free explains the position of many economists today, at least not those at the very top of their profession. Professors Samuelson and Solow, and the other Nobel Laureates who showed up at the White House last October strike one as altogether too liberal and humane. If they were so purely detached, then why were they bothering to make any policy recommendations at all?

146

GATT JUSTICE: WHO GETS THE GAINS OF TRADE?

Or is the problem that they care too much? Many economists, like many scientists, are internationalist at heart; they adopt what Columbia University trade theorist Jagdish Bhagwati refers to as "a cosmopolitan point of view." Their primary allegiance is to the well-being of all people everywhere, not to the members of any particular national group. Like God Himself, they care most about "global welfare." For them, it is enough that global welfare will go up under free trade, even if the welfare of the workers in certain rich countries goes down sharply. After all, is it a tragedy if more American families are forced to go on food stamps when we are helping the many millions of poor wretches who are starving on the streets of Calcutta or Mexico City?

But here again, cosmopolitanism cannot completely explain what needs to be explained, even though it helps. For one thing it is simply dishonest to say that Americans will be better off under free trade, when what is meant is that most Americans will be worse off, even though a few Americans, along with many people overseas, will be better off. When advising a political leader, to confuse these two propositions is worse than dishonest; it is deceitful and borders on treachery. Indeed, in the long run, if it provokes a reaction, it may result in less free trade than a more candid assessment of the situation would have allowed. And it certainly doesn't bode well for the long-run reputation of economists.

THE SEVENTH MILLENNIUM

A better way?

We are left only with a vague but so far
unarticulated feeling that there must be a better way.
Indeed, Professor Samuelson implied as much at the end
of his famous paper, "Protection and Real Wages," in
which the Stolper–Samuelson theorem was first presented
to the world. Having just demonstrated that tariffs could
prop up the wages of workers in a rich country, he
concluded that protection was, nonetheless, not the way to
go. And why not? Because, under free trade, it would
always be possible for the winners to compensate
("bribe") the losers out of their winnings, and leave
everyone better off than before. Yet, as Mr. Samuelson
also observed on a similar occasion, potentiality is not
actuality. The mere fact that, under free trade, it may be
theoretically possible to make everyone better off than
before, if certain additional steps are taken, it is not at all
the same as saying that those steps will (or can) be taken.

Make no mistake. What is required here is nothing
less than a scheme to undo the redistributional effects of
free trade itself. That means taking huge sums of money
out of the pockets of the rich and the powerful and the
politically well connected, and giving it back to ordinary
working people, which is not exactly the sort of
proposition that's wildly popular in Congress these days.

My final conclusion is as inescapable as it is
astonishing. Unless economists have up their sleeves a
practical and politically realistic formula to redistribute

income from the more to the less fortunate members of
society—a formula that could operate on a grand scale
without diminishing the incentives to work, save, and
invest—then they are just blowing so much smoke. For in
the absence of such a formula, it seems clear that the
overwhelming majority of the American people would be
better off if they rejected free trade out of hand. For them
the motto should be "no liberalization without
compensation." They would be better advised to turn to
high tariffs and other impediments to trade with countries
like China and India as the only means available to
protect their livelihoods.

Mr. Samuelson, Mr. Friedman, Mr. Solow, Mr.
Bhagwati: The ball is in your court.

V.
A Note on Wages and Prices

In the neoclassical theory of the firm it is tacitly assumed that wages and prices are determined separately, and indeed quite independently, through competition in labor and commodity markets respectively. Nor does this occasion much surprise since it is in accordance with the conventional practice of the economic world—or, at any rate, of those portions of the economic world that the theory of economics is adapted to serve. Thus, in the case of a typical factory in the manufacturing sector of a modern economy, raw materials are purchased, labor and capital are combined in certain proportions to produce an output, and that output is then turned around and sold. The price of the labor, or wages, is fixed by agreement beforehand through a competitive process in one market, a labor market, while the price of the output is determined subsequently through competition in another market, a commodity market. Under perfect competition, these two markets behave independently; there is no rigid link between them, and the values that prices assume in each for a firm cannot be related in any precise mathematical way.

The purpose of this paper is to point out the possibility in theory of a competitive model in which wages and prices are linked. Such, in particular, would be the case if instead of the traditional fixed-wage contract it

151

were agreed by convention to divide the net product of a firm between labor and capital according to a fixed arithmetic ratio. That is, instead of a fixed hourly wage rate that forms the object of negotiation, a simple ratio would be used: an ordered pair of two numbers, m and n, which divide the net product of the firm (as defined below) into proportional shares on a periodic basis, with m parts going to labor and n parts to capital. Labor's collective share would then be reapportioned among the individual members of the work force on a weighted basis according to the number of hours each worker worked during that period, the skill or experience required, and the degree of difficulty or responsibility of the job he or she performed.

The net product (NP) of a firm for a given period t is defined as the total price of the goods and services produced in that period and subsequently sold, minus all the costs of production (materials, depreciation, shipping, utilities, etc.) except the returns to labor and capital. In other words, it is the value added: the new wealth created by the labor and capital of the firm working jointly during that period.

Under Perfect Competition

Using the same set of assumptions that are explicitly contained in the theory of perfect competition (a sufficient number of independent firms competing in open markets,

A NOTE ON WAGES AND PRICES

uniformity of product, public prices, and so on), we can imagine a self-regulating market economy based entirely, or in part, on the use of such ratios instead of fixed wage rates. How would the ratios be determined? What is the resulting allocation of resources?

The most general rule is that, other things being equal, the ratio in every firm would be established so that at current prices and normal operating capacity (the latter based on the average of an historical time series) the return to capital would be equal to the average prevailing rate of return to capital in the economy as a whole. Likewise for the return to labor: the ratio would be set so that at current prices and normal operating capacity, the remuneration of labor would be equal to the average prevailing rate of remuneration for similarly skilled labor in the economy as a whole.

Ratios that returned more than the prevailing rate would attract capital (or labor), while those that returned less would lose. In mathematical terms

$$\frac{\frac{m}{m+n}(NP)}{L} = w \tag{1}$$

$$\frac{\frac{n}{m+n}(NP)}{C} = r \tag{2}$$

where L is the total number of units of labor employed (weighted for skill), w is the average prevailing rate of wages, C is the value of the capital employed, and r is the average prevailing rate of return to capital.

Under perfect competition, it seems intuitively obvious that equations (1) and (2) would somehow combine with the law of diminishing returns, which is present in the production function of each individual firm to produce an equilibrium in which the relative proportions of labor and capital in every firm are such that

$$MPL = w$$

(3)

$$MPC = r$$

(4)

where MPL is the marginal productivity of labor, and MPC is the marginal productivity of capital.

Yet a proof is nevertheless required. Why? Because in the neoclassical theory of production, it is tacitly assumed that a firm can freely add or subtract units of labor or capital without directly disturbing the wage rates of the rest of the labor force. This is certainly the case when the remuneration of each individual worker is set in the customary way at a fixed hourly rate agreed to ahead of time. But when labor's collective share is determined by a

A NOTE ON WAGES AND PRICES

ratio of the net product, to be reapportioned among the individual workers according to a formula, this assumption no longer holds, and it becomes necessary to adopt a new proof in order to establish these familiar results.

The proof is as follows: Suppose $MPL > w$ for a given firm; then by adding a unit of labor, and choosing a new ratio (m', n') such that

$$\frac{\frac{m'}{m' + n'}(NP + MPL)}{L + 1} = w$$

(5)

which is indifferent to labor, it is possible to increase the rate of return to capital in that firm to a point greater than r. To demonstrate, we begin with a tautology of the form $A/(A+B) = 1 - B/(A+B)$, namely:

$$\frac{\frac{n'}{m' + n'}(NP + MPL)}{C} = \frac{NP + MPL - \frac{m'}{m' + n'}(NP + MPL)}{C}$$

(6)

Multiplying (5) By $L + 1$ and substituting in (6) gives

$$\frac{\frac{n'}{m' + n'}(NP + MPL)}{C} = \frac{NP + MPL - Lw - w}{C}$$

$$(7)$$

Combining equations (1) and (2) and rearranging terms we get

$$Cr = NP - Lw$$

$$(8)$$

Substituting (8) in (7) gives

$$\frac{\frac{n'}{m' + n'}(NP + MPL)}{C} = \frac{Cr + (MPL - w)}{C}$$

$$(9)$$

But since $MPL > w$, therefore $MPL - w > 0$, which implies

$$\frac{Cr + (MPL - w)}{C} > \frac{Cr}{C} = r$$

$$(10)$$

Substituting (10) in (9) gives

$$\frac{\frac{n'}{m' + n'}(NP + MPL)}{C} > r$$

$$(11)$$

which is the desired result. Likewise, if $MPL < w$ or $MPC \neq r$, it is possible to either subtract a unit of labor or add or subtract a unit of capital and choose a new ratio (m', n'), which is indifferent to labor, but which increases the rate of return to capital in the firm to a point greater than r. The demonstration in each case is analogous to the above.

We conclude, therefore, that under perfect competition, an economy based on ratios instead of fixed wage rates is formally equivalent to the neoclassical model as regards the allocation of resources and the distribution of income.

Under Imperfect Competition

The interest of these ratios lies not in the ideal world of perfect competition, however. Rather, it lies in the real world of imperfect competition where large-scale organizations of labor and capital are found and where market forces break down under monopoly power. It is here that we can expect an economy based on ratios to differ in a number of significant ways from one based on conventional wage contracts. Without trying to explore them in any detail, let me simply note what some of these differences are.

THE SEVENTH MILLENNIUM

1. Economies based on ratios would not experience the downward stickiness of wages, which has traditionally contributed to the business cycle and is one of the main justifications for a monetary policy of inflation, as advocated by Milton Friedman and John Maynard Keynes, for example.[40] By the same token, commodity prices would also be more downwardly flexible once capital holders do not bear the entire burden of price reductions.

2. Reductions in employment and earnings during a downturn in the business cycle could be equitably shared by all the workers in a firm instead of falling disproportionately on a few who lose their jobs completely. Not only would everyone's wages automatically fall together as a consequence of the decrease in demand for the product they produce, but any residual decline in the volume of employment could be shared by shortening the workweek.

3. The cost-push mechanism of price inflation would no longer operate. Cost-push is a phenomenon, last seen in the 1970s, that occurs when strong labor unions negotiate cost-of-living adjustments in their wages to reflect rises in the general price level. These adjustments are then passed on by their employers in the form of further price increases. Using (m, n) ratios, however, cost-of-living adjustments would no longer be necessary, since

increases in commodity prices would automatically be reflected by increases in nominal wages.[41]

4. With (m, n) ratios it is likely there would be a natural evolution toward greater worker participation in the design and organization of production. In other words, there would be a tendency toward greater workplace democracy, not at the level of the parent corporation, but at the level of the individual production facility. Innovations on the factory floor that increase the efficiency of the production process should be more common once those who are closest to the process of production, the front-line workers themselves, have a direct financial stake in the outcome.

5. With (m, n) ratios we could conceivably see two identical factories owned by the same parent in price competition with each other. This might occur, for instance, if the workers in each facility demand a say in where prices are set, and hence in what the local wage-rate and volume of employment would be.

6. With (m, n) ratios large multi-national companies would no longer be so free to engage in artificial transfer prices as a way to avoid their taxes in the country of origin. This is because artificially low transfer prices would adversely affect the wages of the workers involved. Transparency in all not-at-arms-length transactions would be required.

7. With (m, n) ratios there would be an empirical basis for arbitration between labor and capital in those cases in which a mutually agreeable ratio cannot be negotiated through collective bargaining. To see why, consider the situation under perfect competition. By definition, with (m, n) ratios, wages and profits would be described by equations (1) and (2) above:

$$\frac{\frac{m}{m+n}(NP)}{L} = w \tag{1}$$

$$\frac{\frac{n}{m+n}(NP)}{C} = r \tag{2}$$

When we combine these two equations, they yield

$$\frac{Lw}{Cr} = \frac{m}{n} \tag{12}$$

in which L, w, C, and r are all empirical terms: L is the quantity (and grades) of labor employed, C is the quantity of capital employed, and w and r are the average prevailing rates of return for labor (in its various grades) and capital respectively in the economy as a whole. In other words, all four of these variables can be estimated using empirical data with a tolerable degree of precision.[42]

VI.

A One Parameter Graduated Expenditure Tax

While the theoretical virtues and practical difficulties of a graduated expenditure tax are well known (Fisher,[43], Kaldor,[44] Merriam[45]), less attention has been paid to the number of parameters required to fully specify such a tax. Here we describe a single-parameter version of a graduated expenditure tax that is at once simple, transparent, and continuously progressive over the entire range of consumer spending.

For a given society's unit of currency, let the integer n denote the total number of units of spending for a given taxpayer in a given tax period. We then specify the parameter m (a very small number of order 10^{-6}) to be the marginal tax rate applied to the first unit of expenditure, $2m$ the marginal rate applied to the second unit, $3m$ the marginal rate applied to the third, and so on. In other words, instead of being arbitrarily defined the way they are now, every tax bracket is exactly one unit of currency wide and the marginal tax rates on successive brackets form an arithmetic sequence, each term of which increases by the amount of the parameter m.

With this information in hand, it is an easy matter to compute every taxpayer's total tax liability (which we denote with the lowercase letter t) using the formula for the sum of an arithmetic sequence that we all learned in high school, namely:

$$tn = \frac{mn(n + 1)}{2}$$

where tn denotes the total tax owed on n units of spending in a given tax period.

We assume the parameter m can be adjusted ("tuned") by the taxing authority depending on the target revenue it aims to raise, which we denote with the capital letter T. Then for a given society's current distributions of income and wealth and its propensities to consume (all of which can be estimated on the basis of recent historical experience, assuming such a tax was in place in the preceding tax periods), m is clearly a function of T. In other words, once the target revenue has been set, there are no free parameters to be put in by hand.

To get a sense of what such a tax would look like in practice, consider the United States as it exists today. Here the unit of currency is the dollar, and for purposes of illustration, we choose the parameter m, the marginal tax rate applied to the first dollar of consumer spending, to be exactly 6×10^{-6}. The graphs below plot the total tax individual taxpayers would owe on personal expenditures ranging from \$10,000 to \$2,000,000 in a given tax period.

164

A ONE PARAMETER GRADUATED
EXPENDITURE TAX

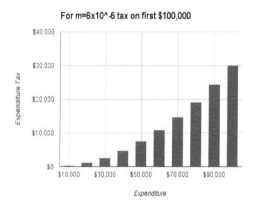

Figure 5

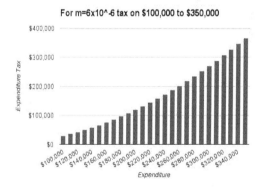

Figure 6

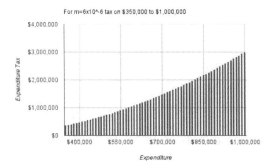

Figure 7

VII.

A One Parameter Earned Income Tax Credit

As a companion to the single parameter graduated expenditure tax, we here describe a one parameter version of the earned income tax credit, only in this case, the marginal tax credits that apply to successive units of earned income form a geometric as opposed to an arithmetic sequence (differ by a common ratio as opposed to a common sum).

Thus for a given unit of currency, let ε be a very small number of order 10^{-5}. We then define $1 - \varepsilon$ to be the tax credit a wage worker receives for the first unit of currency he earns in a given tax period, $(1 - \varepsilon)^2$ the credit he receives for the second unit of currency earned, $(1 - \varepsilon)^3$ the credit for the third unit, and so on. It is then a simple matter to compute a wage worker's total tax credit for that period using the formula for the sum of a geometric sequence that we all learned in high school, namely:

$$\mathbf{t}_{cr}^n = \frac{(1 - \varepsilon) - (1 - \varepsilon)^{n+1}}{\varepsilon}$$

where $\mathbf{t}_{cr}^n$ denotes the total tax credit on n units of wages received.

To get a sense of what this version of an earned income tax credit would look like in practice, consider the

167

United States as it exists today. Here the unit of currency is the dollar, and for purposes of illustration, we choose the parameter ε to be exactly 5×10^{-5}. The table and chart below show what the total credits would be, both absolutely and as a percentage of wages, for workers earning between $5000 and $100,000 a year.

Earnings	Tax Credit	Credit as % of Earnings
$5,000	$4,424	88%
$10,000	$7,869	79%
$20,000	$12,642	63%
$30,000	$15,537	52%
$40,000	$17,203	43%
$50,000	$18,357	37%
$60,000	$19,003	32%
$70,000	$19,395	28%
$80,000	$19,633	25%
$90,000	$19,777	22%
$100,000	$19,864	20%

A ONE PARAMETER EARNED INCOME TAX
CREDIT

Figure 8

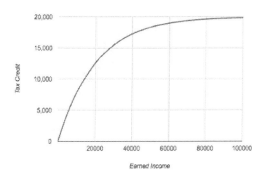

EITC when parameter e is set equal to 5 x 10^-5)

Figure 9

Discussion

The first thing we note is that the lower a worker's total earnings, the larger his tax credit will be as a percentage of those earnings. In this it resembles the current earned income tax credit (EITC) and is in keeping with the purpose of an earned income tax credit, namely, to enable low-income workers to enjoy significantly higher standards of living than their market wages alone can support.

On the other hand, we also note an anomaly: unlike today, workers whose total earnings are the highest and

169

who, presumably, are least in need of a subsidy, would in fact receive the biggest credits of all in absolute amount. There is no threshold beyond which the size of their credits begins to decline.

This anomaly can be reduced, however, and in some cases eliminated completely if there were also in place a one parameter graduated expenditure tax like the one we previously constructed. For two reasons:

First, because as a rule, workers who earn more will also consume more and will therefore face higher marginal tax rates on any part of their credits they use to further increase their consumption. Thus, even though the size of their credits would be larger absolutely, its after-tax purchasing power in the present tax period (and quite likely in future periods as well) would be less, in some cases much less.

And second, because additional revenue will be required to finance this (or any) system of earned income tax credits, which means that the parameter m would have to be dialed up to increase the marginal tax rates on consumption. And since by definition those rates increase arithmetically over the entire range of consumer spending, workers whose earnings are too high will as a rule choose or (if their propensities to save are too low, but not less than zero) actually be forced to consume less than they did before the system of credits became law. For them, "what the right hand giveth, the left hand taketh away."

Or to put it another way, for any value of ε there exists an earnings threshold, call it point p, beyond which

A ONE PARAMETER EARNED INCOME TAX
CREDIT

a wage worker's disposable income becomes less *even after receiving his credit*. Where that threshold lies is an empirical question the answer to which will vary depending upon a society's distributions of income and wealth, the distribution of its propensities to consume, and the revenues it requires for other public purposes. Without any data, the most we can say is that, these four variables being held constant, the closer the parameter ε is to zero the higher the parameter m must be set to raise the necessary revenues, and therefore the lower that threshold will be.

We leave it to mathematical economists to describe the range of possible inequalities of consumption in a society as a function of these variables.

End Notes

1. Revelations 21:4.

2. *"well out beyond the exurban fringe"*: Even though the new towns will be at a considerable distance from the nearest major metropolitan center, they will nonetheless remain within the metropolitan matrix. Which is to say, they will continue to rely on the nearest big city for a variety of different kinds of material support: for industrial services of all kinds, managerial talent, technical assistance, wholesale storage and distribution, municipal finance, major medical care, basic scientific research and development, etc. For these reasons, the new towns might best be conceptualized not as a rejection of the city as such, but rather as the third and likely last stage in the suburbanization of the metropolitan complex.

3. *"all those doing routine wage work"*: Factory managers, by contrast, are not presumed to be part-time. Nor will factory managers necessarily be permanent members of the communities in which they reside, which is especially likely should they be in the direct employ of outside corporations or groups of investors whose interests they are paid to represent. The number of such outside managers will vary greatly depending on the skills and talents of the

173

local population, and they are likely to be housed separately in their own parts of town.

4. *"to which, presumably, we are adapted by nature."*: This refers to what evolutionary psychologists have come to call *the environment of evolutionary adaptation* (or EEA), formerly known as the Paleolithic or Old Stone Age. See Barkow, Cosmides, and Tooby.

5. Revelations 2:4–5.

6. For a good overview see "What is New Urbanism" on the Congress for the New Urbanism website: https://tinyurl.com/ugsyg8r.

7. See Ebenezer Howard, *Garden Cities of Tomorrow*.

8. See Henry George, *Progress and Poverty*.

9. Alexis de Tocqueville, *Democracy in America, Volume I*.

10. Among many other things, Rouse is famous for his dictum that "the answer to bad development is good development." See Joshua Olsen's *Better Places, Better Lives: A Biography of James Rouse*.

11. See *Frederick Law Olmsted: Plans and Views of Public Parks*. See also *Frederick Law Olmstead: Writings on Landscape, Culture, and Society* (Library of America, no. 270).

END NOTES

12. See Matthew 14: 14–30. Jesus's parable of the talents is a remarkably clear statement of the law of capital markets as it operates on Wall Street and elsewhere in the field of mergers and acquisitions, upon which the efficiency of modern capitalism depends. Put another way, should manufacturers employing incentive-based work sprints as described in this chapter turn out to be significantly more profitable in fact as well as in theory, then their competitors will be forced to follow suit in order to survive. However, this will only be the case if protective tariffs are in place that close off the possibility of their shifting operations to low-wage countries overseas.

13. See Bernard Bailyn's *The Barbarous Years: The Peopling of British North America: 1600–1675*).

14. For an entertaining overview see Robert Heilbroner's *The Earthly Philosophers*.

15. For a full accounting of the horrors of Marxism-Leninism in action, see Nicolas Werth et al., *The Black Book of Communism: Crimes, Terror, Repression.*

16. See Stanley Jevons, *The Theory of Political Economy.*

17. See Lincoln, James F., *A New Approach to Industrial Economics.*

18. See Daniel Bell's *The Coming of Post-Industrial Society*.

19. See Appendix V for the story of how this legislative change came about.

20. See the *2018 Small Business Profile* published by the U.S. Small Business Administration: https://tinyurl.com/vgh2wbh.

21. Luke 14:28.

22. For a good overview see AECOM's *Garden towns and villages cost model*: https://tinyurl.com/yc7wfpbn.

23. See HomeGuide's "How Much Does It Cost to Build a House?": https://tinyurl.com/yb4k2oq6.

24. Hawthorne, Nathaniel, Mosses from an Old Manse (James R. Osgood and Sons, 1873) p. 17.

25. See Max Weber's *Theory of Social and Economic Organization* (Oxford University Press, 1947).

26. Concerning the power of austerity to foster a sense of community, whenever I try to imagine the kinds of demands that might be placed on future generations of teenagers who are just coming of age in one of these new country towns, the only thing that comes to mind are rites of passage that mirror the physical and moral hardships that generations of our ancestors were forced to endure in order to make the new way

176

of life possible. Nothing so cruel as a stairway of death to be sure, but perhaps a succession of twelve-to-fourteen-hour days doing stoop labor under a hot summer sun, or something equally painful.

27. Romans 12:5.

28. See Avner Greif, "Family Structure, Institutions, and Growth: The Origins and Implications of Western Corporations" (*American Economic Review*, Volume 96, no. 2, May 2006).

29. On the prohibition of consanguineous forms of marriage see the blog post, "whatever happened to european tribes?" by HBD CHICK: https://tinyurl.com/qfm3k2e. See also "The Cousin Marriage Conundrum" by Steve Sailer: https://tinyurl.com/ydxetyjh.

30. *"as it can be understood in the Judeo-Christian tradition upon which our civilization was founded"*: This clause needs to be parsed very carefully. As it *can* be understood does not mean as it can *only* be understood. Ours is but one possible interpretation of that religious tradition which, we argue, is consistent with scripture. We should not and do not deny the existence of other interpretations that are equally consistent, at least one of which, let us hope, is equally true. Nor does it mean that there are not other traditions, not all of them necessarily Biblical in origin, that share the same basic goal, secular

humanism being the most obvious example (notwithstanding the fact that three of its most cherished ideals—of political freedom, social justice, and human equality—are arguably Biblical in origin). Islam may be another example. Not sure about Hinduism, Taoism, Buddhism, or other East Asian religious traditions.

31. *"dazzling displays of intellectual brilliance that serve only to blind even as they fail to illuminate"*: Paul Samuelson, Noam Chomsky, and Jacques Derrida furnish three notable examples of what I am warning against here. Rare talents like Alexander Hamilton, on the other hand, who manage to be both brilliant and illuminating at the same time should definitely be listened to, even though another Franklin or Lincoln would be even better on account of their more commonsense way of expressing themselves.

32. See Walter Laqueur, *A History of Zionism*.

33. See Joel Garreau, *The Nine Nations of North America*.

34. See Paul Conkin, Tomorrow a New World: The New Deal Community Program (Cornell 1959).

35. See Samuel Gompers, *Labor and the Common Welfare* (Beaufort, 1969).

36. See Caves and Jones, *World Trade and Payments* for the classic teaching text. See also Stolper and

END NOTES

Samuelson's famous essay, "Protection and Real
Wages," which caused a great stir when it was
published in 1942. For the original demonstration of
the need to compensate whole factors of production
in a world composed of rich and poor countries, see
Swedish economist Eli Heckscher's groundbreaking
1920 essay, "The Effect of Foreign Trade on the
Distribution of Income."

37. *"a balance of power between land and labor on the
one side and capital on the other"*: Such a balance
presumes similar levels of organization on both sides
of the equation. To establish such parity, I foresee the
emergence of a new clerisy or counter-elite based in
the towns and organized along Presbyterian lines, one
of whose responsibilities will be to represent the
towns in their collective bargaining with capital. To
avoid a conflict of interest here while taking into
account the so-called iron law of oligarchy, it is
essential that the aggregate income of this new
clerisy be proportional to average hourly earnings of
the workers it represents. In addition to its collective
bargaining responsibilities, this new clerisy would
also be in charge of primary and secondary education
in the towns as well as the liberal arts colleges and
universities in which its own members would be
educated. When we consider the overproduction of
elites in the United States today—the fact that there
are so many more university graduates with advanced
degrees than there are opportunities for them to find

employment in their chosen fields of study—it seems likely that a large pool of potential recruits to such a new corporate body already exists.

38. *Hanifya* in the Koran. For details in its historical and sociological context, see my essay "The Torah and the West Bank" (*Judaism: A Quarterly Journal of Jewish Life and Thought* Vol. 36, no. 3, Summer Issue 1987).

39. The possibilities in this area have yet to be explored. See Appendices VI and VII for a path to possible implementation.

40. See Keynes, John Maynard, *The General Theory of Employment, Money, and Interest* (Macmillan, 1936). This particular point is brought home in the very first chapter, where Keynes draws a distinction between nominal and real hourly wage rates.

41. MIT economist Martin Weitzman convincingly argues this point in his book, *The Share Economy: Combating Stagflation* (Harvard University Press, 1986).

42. But see Oskar Morgenstern's *On the Accuracy of Economic Observations,* an important book that deserves more attention than it has received so far. Measurements without error bars are at best misleading, if not the sign of a pseudoscience, and yet one rarely sees the range of uncertainty in the data with which economists deal.

END NOTES

43. Fisher, Irving, Constructive Income Taxation: A Proposal for Reform (Harper & Brothers, 1942).

44. Kaldor, Nicholas, *An Expenditure Tax* (George, Allen, and Unwin, 1956) is an excellent overview of the entire subject.

45. Merriam, et al., *The Expenditure Tax: Concept, Administration, and Possible Applications* (Advisory Commission on Intergovernmental Relations, Washington, D.C., 1974).

Select Bibliography

AECOM, "Garden towns and villages cost model," https://tinyurl.com/tyh7vlk

Alexander, Christopher, *A Pattern Language: Towns, Buildings, Construction* (Oxford University Press, 1977)

Boehm, Christopher, *Hierarchy in the Forest: The Evolution of Egalitarian Behavior* (Harvard University Press, 2001)

Caves, Richard and Ronald Jones, *World Trade and Payments, Sixth Edition* (Harper Collins, 1993)

Conkin, Paul K, *Tomorrow a New World: The New Deal Community Program* (Cornell, 1959)

Emerson, Ralph Waldo, *Essays and Lectures* (New American Library, 1983)

Fisher, Irving, *Constructive Income Taxation: A Proposal for Reform* (Harper & Brothers, 1942)

Friedman, Milton, *Notes on Lectures in Price Theory* (University of Chicago, 1960)

Galbraith, John Kenneth *American Capitalism: The Concept of Countervailing Power* (Martino Fine Books, 2012)

Garreau, Joel, *The Nine Nations of North America*, (Houghton Mifflin, 1981)

George, Henry, *Progress and Poverty* (D. Appleton and Company, New York, 1886)

Gompers, Samuel, *Labor and the Common Welfare* (Beaufort, 1969)

Hamilton, Alexander, James Madison, and John Jay, *The Federalist Papers* (Everyman's Library, 1961)

Hawthorne, Nathaniel, *Mosses from an Old Manse* (Modern Library Classics, 2003)

Heckscher, Eli F., "The Effect of Foreign Trade on the Distribution of Income," *Ekonomisk Tidskrift* 21: 497–512, (Uppsala, 1920), English translation in *Heckscher-Ohlin Trade Theory* (MIT Press, 1991)

Heilbroner, Robert, *The Worldly Philosophers* (Simon and Schuster, 1953)

Herzl, Theodor, *The Jewish State* (Dover Publishing, 1989)

Howard, Ebenezer, *Garden Cities of Tomorrow* (MIT Press, 1965)

Huntington, Samuel, *American Politics: The Promise of Disharmony* (Harvard University Press, 1981)

James, William, *The Will to Believe and Other Essays* (Longmans, 1909)

184

SELECT BIBLIOGRAPHY

Jevons, Stanley, *The Theory of Political Economy* (Oxford University Press, 1909)

Kaldor, Nicholas, *An Expenditure Tax* (Routledge, 2003)

Kay, David Johnston, *Perfectly Legal* (Portfolio, 2003)

Keynes, John Maynard, *The General Theory of Employment, Interest and Money* (Macmillan, 1936)

Keynes, John Maynard, "Economic Possibilities for Our Grandchildren" in *Essays in Persuasion* (Macmillan, 1931)

Laqueur, Walter, *A History of Zionism* (Schocken, 2003)

Lea, Luke, "A Communitarian Prospect," *Dissent* (Winter, 1985)

Lea, Luke, "GATT Justice: Who Gets the Gains of Trade," *Challenge* (Volume 37, 1994)

Lea, Luke, "The Torah and the West Bank," *Judaism: A Quarterly Journal of Jewish Life and Opinion* (Volume 36, Summer Issue, 1987)

Lincoln, James F., *A New Approach to Industrial Economics* (The Devon-Adair Company, 1961)

Lovins, Amory, *Soft Energy Paths: Towards a Durable Peace* (Harper Colophon Books, 1979)

Madison, James, *Notes of Debates in the Federal Convention of 1787* (Ohio University Press, 1987)

Morgenstern, Oskar, *On the Accuracy of Economic Observations, Second Edition, Completely Revised* (Princeton University Press, 1963)

Mumford, Lewis, *The City in History* (Harcourt Brace Jovanovich, 1961)

Murray, Charles, "A Place for Everyone," concluding chapter of *The Bell Curve: Intelligence and Class Structure in American Life* (The Free Press, 1994)

Olsen, Joshua, *Better Places, Better Lives: A Biography of James Rouse* (Urban Land Institute, 2004)

Paterson, Isabel, *The God of the Machine* (Transaction Publishers, 1993)

Popper, Karl, *The Open Society and Its Enemies*, Volume 2 (Princeton University Press, 1962)

Ricardo, David, *The Principles of Political Economy and Taxation* (Everyman's Library, Dutton, 1973)

Rybczynski, Witold, *The Most Beautiful House in the World* (Penguin Books, 1990)

Samuelson, Paul, "International Trade and the Equalization of Factor Prices," (*The Economic Journal*, 1948)

Seligman, Ben, *Main Currents in Modern Economics* (Transaction Publishers, 1990)

SELECT BIBLIOGRAPHY

Smith, Adam, *The Wealth of Nations* (Modern Library, 1965)

Stark, Rodney, *The Victory of Reason: How Christianity Led to Freedom, Capitalism, and Western Success* (Random House, 2006)

Stolper, W.F. and P.A. Samuelson, "Protection and Real Wages," (*Review of Economic Studies*, 9: 58–73, 1942)

Tocqueville, Alexis de, *Democracy in America* (Schocken Books, 1961)

Unwin, Raymond and Walter Creese, *The Legacy of Raymond Unwin: A Human Pattern for Planning* (MIT Press, 1967)

Ward, Barbara, *The Rich Nations and the Poor Nations* (W. W. Norton & Co., 1962)

Weber, Max, *The Protestant Ethic and the Spirit of Capitalism: and Other Writings* (Penguin, 2002)

Weber, Max, *The Theory of Social and Economic Organization* (Oxford University Press, 1947)

Weber, Max, *The Vocation Lectures: Science as a Vocation, Politics as a Vocation* (Hackett, 2004)

Weizmann, Chaim, *Trial and Error* (Harper, 1949)

Winthrop, John, *A Model of Christian Charity* (Passerino, 2020)

THE SEVENTH MILLENNIUM

Acknowledgements

I wish to express my deepest gratitude to my former wife, Patricia Lea, without whose long-suffering tolerance of her husband's obsession none of these pages could ever have been written. I would also like to thank my cousin, Gordon Smith, who showed me how to raise the money I needed to pay for the Gallup poll I commissioned in 1976, the results of which are what determined me to continue pursuing this project despite my family's misgivings. Robert Lekachman, Robert Heilbroner, Milton Friedman, and Irving Howe are three economists and an editor who gave me encouragement along the way, as did Abraham Feinstein, my rabbi and mentor at Mizpah Congregation. Last but not least I want to acknowledge the loyal support of J. Robert McGuff, whose patronage over many years gave me the leisure I needed to develop the ideas in this book. He was a true centurion.

About the Author

Luke Lea was born in Chattanooga, Tennessee, in 1942. He attended Reed College, Johns Hopkins University, and the University of Tubingen, concentrating in literature and mathematics. He lives in Walden, Tennessee, a small town in Southern Appalachia, which is where his mother's side of the family is from, his father's being from New England by way of Ohio.

Index

INDEX

civilization
  Western, 29, 81
  Chinese, 81, 82
  archaic forms of, 81
  comparative history of, 94
class (social)
  entrepreneurial, 104
  labor vs. capital, 105,
  working class, 4, 8, 42, 51, 74, 75,
    100, 135, 143, 148
classical economics, 131–133
classical physics, 133
clerisy, new
  as counter-elite, 179
  based in the towns 179
  organized along Presbyterian
    lines, 179
  collective bargaining role, 179
  remuneration based on, 179
  in charge of primary and
    secondary education, 179
  and the overproduction of elites
    179–180
  and the iron law of oligarchy, 179
Clinton, William, 127, 142–143
Cold War, 127
collective bargaining
  right of, 85
  need for, 32, 58, 160, 179
  using (m, n) ratios, 160–161
  role of the new clerisy in, 147
colleges (and universities)
  community, 89, 90
  liberal arts, 70, 94–95, 179
  failure of existing, 94
  need for new, 94–95
  and the overproduction of elites,
    179
college towns, 121
communism, 30, 82, 127, 140, 175
community
  definition of, 78
  traditional, 78
  intentional, 29–30, 78
  requirements for political and
    economic independence of,
    121–122, 124

importance of austerity in building
    a strong sense of community,
    78–79
commuter towns, 121
comparative advantage, 101, 130–
    132, 139
compensation, principle of, 140, 148
compensation, workers', 124
competition
  and the off-shoring of
    manufacturing, 51, 52
  effect of tariffs on, 52, 130, 132,
    141, 147, 148, 175
  for housing in safe neighborhoods
    with good public schools, 73
  between factories owned by the
    same parent company, 131
computers and the new information
  technology
  new voting procedures made
    possible by, 87
  eroding the relative advantage of
    big cities, 28
concordance of classes, 105
conflicts of interest
  within the new country towns,
    123, 125, 179
  in existing society, 91, 99
  between capital and the new
    country towns, 58, 124, 179
  between labor and capital, 58,
    105, 143, 157, 160, 179
  see also iron law of oligarchy, 148
Congress, US, role of, 52, 97, 99, 104,
    142
consumption, progressive tax on,
    103–104, 170–171
corporation(s)
  legal definition of, 81
  distinguishing feature of Western
    civilization, 81
  historical importance of, 82
  forms of, 82
  the right to organize, 82
  advantage of, 82
  American Zionist organization as a
    new kind of corporation, 82–83

INDEX

197

INDEX

INDEX

INDEX

and the rule of austerity, 74
  under a graduated expenditure
    tax, 103–104
Scripture, quotations, 1, 5, 29, 61, 81
secular humanism, 177–178
self-government, 17, 24, 25–26
serfs, 99
service economy, end of, 51
services, personal
  in the new country towns, 3
  concept of a post-service
    economy, 51
share economy, concept of, 151–152
  under perfect competition, 152–
    157
  under imperfect competition,
    157–161
  macroeconomic theory of, 158
  and incentive-based work sprints,
    32
  see also profit sharing
sharing, role of in the new neighborhood communities, 12–13
shell corporations, need to abolish,
  103
shopping, retail
  distances from home, 22, 23
  neighborhood convenience stores,
    23
  in downtown commercial district,
    25, 26
  and the new information
    technology, 27
shopping malls
  James Rouse's concept of, 25
  vs. traditional town squares, 25
  a new hybrid architectural form,
    25
  abandoned malls as ideal local
    chapter locations, 88
sidewalks, 23, 68
simple life, ideal of, *see* preface
site acquisition, 19, 20
six-hour day, 102–103
Smith, Adam, 30, 101, 129, 132, 141
social classes

conflicts of interest, 91, 100, 105,
  120, 148
Ciceronian ideal, 105
Social Security, crisis of, 8–10
Solow, Robert, 149
standard of living
  measuring, 23, 76–77
  personal transportation, cost of,
    19, 24
  standard of living vs. quality of life,
    76–77
  revealed preference only way to
    compare, 77
state and local chapters, 87
state capitals, 121
Steelcase, Inc., 45, 54
subsidies (of wages)
  theoretical justification, 104, 147–
    148
  and the principle of compensation,
    104
  with an earned income tax credit,
    104
  under a single parameter version
    of the earned income tax credit,
    137–141
suburbanization (of the metropolitan
  complex), 173

T

tariffs (effects of), 52, 132, 147, 148,
  175
  see also protectionism
taxation
  on income, 103
  on consumption, 103,
  on commercial real estate, 24
  on capital gains, interest, estates,
    corporations, sales, etc., 103
  concept of a graduated
    expenditure tax, 103, 163–166
tax havens, need to abolish, 103
techniques of mass production, 5, 31
  standardization of product, 31
  division of labor, 31
  economies of scale, 31

205

Made in the USA
Columbia, SC
07 September 2020